Prescriptive Reasoning

*Essays on Logic as
the Art of Reasoning Well*

Richard L. Epstein

ARF

Advanced Reasoning Forum

For more information contact:
   Advanced Reasoning Forum
   P. O. Box 635
   Socorro, NM 87801   USA
   www.ARFbooks.org

paperback ISBN 978-0-9834521-4-0
e-book ISBN 978-0-9834521-5-7

Prescriptive Reasoning

Essays on Logic as the Art of Reasoning Well

Richard L. Epstein

In the discussions of the wise there is found unrolling and rolling up, convincing and conceding; agreements and disagreements are reached. And in all that the wise suffer no disturbance.   Nagasena

Essays on Logic as the Art of Reasoning Well

Dedicated to

Fred Kroon

with much gratitude for his criticisms, encouragement,
and friendship for many years

Preface

This series of books presents the fundamentals of logic in a style accessible to both students and scholars. The text of each essay presents a story, the main line of development of the ideas, while the notes and appendices place the research within a larger scholarly context. The essays overlap, forming a unified analysis of logic as the art of reasoning well. In order that they may be read independently, there is repetition of some material among them.

The topic of this volume is prescriptive reasoning. Descriptive claims say how the world is, was, or will be; prescriptive claims say how the world should be. We have fairly clear rules for reasoning with descriptive claims. The goal of the first essay, "Reasoning with Prescriptive Claims," is to clarify how to reason with prescriptive ones. The first step in doing so is to justify viewing prescriptions as true or false.

That justification is part of a general approach to reasoning in which many kinds of evaluations are taken to be true/false divisions. That view has been implicit if not explicit in analyses of reasoning from formal logic through argument analysis. In "Truth and Reasoning" I set out reasons for adopting that methodology.

Theories, too, seem to be descriptive or prescriptive. Some say how the world is, others how the world should be. Yet as I show in "Prescriptive Theories?", on close examination the distinction evaporates. Unless, that is, one says that certain theories about values use an entirely different notion of truth than is used in science and is codified in our usual methods of reasoning. Absent that, there seems to be no justification for constructing and evaluating differently what are typically thought of as prescriptive theories

Many discussions of how to evaluate prescriptive claims are given in terms of what is rational or irrational to do. In the final essay, "Rationality," I look at what we mean by the idea of someone being rational and show the limitations of that label in evaluating reasoning or actions.

I hope in this book to give a clearer idea of how to reason about what should be done. But even if we understand that quite well, what should be done is a question beyond logic.

Acknowledgments

Many people have helped me over the years I have been working on this material. William S. Robinson and Fred Kroon, in particular, have given much of their time and thought to suggestions that have improved all these essays. They and the other members of the Advanced Reasoning Forum have helped me to understand the issues here, and I am grateful to all of them. I am also grateful to Jack Birner for comments on a draft of "Reasoning with Prescriptive Claims" and to Ronald De Sousa for his comments on "Rationality." I am thankful, too, for the suggestions which David Isles made for "Reasoning with Prescriptive Claims" and Lou Gobles for his comments on the appendix of that essay. The suggestions of Paul Livingston on what I had thought was a nearly final draft of the entire book helped me see many problems that I hope to have corrected or at least made clearer, and I am grateful to him. The mistakes, however, remain mine.

Publishing history of the essays in this volume

The essay "Reasoning with Prescriptive Claims" was motivated by discussions with members of the Advanced Reasoning Forum. This is its first publication.

This is also the first publication of "Prescriptive Theories?".

And this is the first publication of "Truth and Reasoning," too, though parts of it have appeared in my other writings.

"Rationality" was the keynote address of the first meeting of the Advanced Reasoning Forum. It was published as an appendix to my *Five Ways of Saying "Therefore."* A discussion of the notion of rationality for actions has been added, and the notes have been expanded to include comparisons to more views of rationality. This version appears also in *The Fundamentals of Argument Analysis*.

Reasoning with Prescriptive Claims

Descriptive claims say how the world is, was, or will be.
Prescriptive claims say how the world should be. We have fairly
clear rules for reasoning with descriptive claims. The goal of
this essay is to clarify how to reason with prescriptive claims.

Introduction

Descriptive claims say how the world is, was, or will be. Prescriptive claims say how the world should be. For example,

Descriptive:
> Drunken drivers kill more people than sober drivers do.
> Dick is cold.
> Selling cocaine is against the law.

Prescriptive:
> There needs to be a law against drunken driving.
> Dick ought to put his sweater on.
> Ian shouldn't sell cocaine.

We have fairly clear rules for reasoning with descriptive claims. Our goal here is to clarify how to reason with prescriptive claims.

The first problem is whether prescriptive sentences are indeed claims, that is, are true or false. I argue in Section A that how we conceive of truth and how we reason with descriptive claims are compatible with ascribing truth or falsity to prescriptive sentences. That section also establishes the background for the two methods of reasoning with prescriptive claims that follow.

We often look for fundamental standards to justify the truth or falsity of prescriptive claims. In Section B we'll consider what rules for reasoning we can employ when we do so.

In contrast, we often decide whether a prescriptive claim is true or false by asking whether the prescribed action fulfills an aim. We'll see how we can analyze prescriptive claims that way in Section C.

The two methods illuminate different aspects of how we can or should reason with prescriptive claims. We relate them in Section D by seeing that the direction of inference of each is the reverse of the other.

Other approaches to reasoning with prescriptive claims are briefly surveyed in an appendix.

A. General Background

1. "Should"

One way we make prescriptions is with the word "should":

> You should close the window.
> Dick should get a job.
> We shouldn't kill dogs.

Each of these sentences is a suggestion, advice, or perhaps command. This is the basic sense of simple prescriptive sentences: to suggest, advise, or command someone to do something. This use of "should" is quite different from using "should" to indicate likelihood, as in "Dick should be here about noon," which is not prescriptive.

Let's first try to sort out how to reason with sentences that use "should" in the sense of advice, in the hope that our methods will generalize to other prescriptions.

2. Claims, advice, and truth

The goal of reasoning is to determine what is true and what follows from various assumptions. Our first consideration in investigating prescriptive sentences then is whether we can indeed view them as being true or false.

Perhaps it's wrong to view prescriptions as true or false. Perhaps they are only good or bad, apt or inappropriate. In that case, the rules we have for reasoning with descriptive claims don't apply. But consider two examples.

Example 1   Physician: Don't smoke anymore.
Matilda: O.K.

Analysis   The physician has stated an imperative ("command" seems too strong a word). Suppose Matilda then goes out and smokes a couple cigarettes. We'd say she's perverse, or stupid, or she just didn't follow the doctor's orders. There's no question of belief or truth.

Example 2   Physician: You shouldn't smoke anymore.
Matilda: I agree.

Analysis   Suppose again that Matilda goes out and smokes a couple cigarettes. In this case we think she can be charged with inconsistency (if she hasn't changed her mind). That's because Matilda's attitude about "You shouldn't smoke" is one of belief. The doctor is not commanding her; such a conversation would typically be preceded or followed by an attempt by the doctor to convince her that she shouldn't smoke. And belief is belief that something is true.

Perhaps, though, what Matilda is asked to believe is that the prescriptive claim is good advice. But to say that "You should stop smoking" is good advice is just to say that you should stop smoking. The label "good advice," like "true" for descriptive claims, adds nothing.

This suggests that we can ask under what conditions a prescriptive claim is good advice, that is, when someone is justified in following its recommendation. Once we do that, we might as well say that those are the conditions for the claim to be true. We just delete the phrase "is good advice": "These are the conditions under which you are justified in believing the prescriptive claim ~~is good advice~~."[1]

With descriptive claims what is true is not false, what is false is not true. That seems not only apt but obvious when we think of truth in terms of some kind of correspondence with a world external to us. But why should dividing prescriptions into good advice and bad advice be mutually exclusive? Why can't we have a prescription that is both good advice and bad advice?

If a sentence such as "You should never torture a dog" is both good advice and bad advice, then we are enjoined to believe and not to believe, to do and not to do, to act and not to act. That we cannot do. Perhaps such dilemmas are real. Perhaps our reasoning will lead us to them in some cases. But if so, there's no reason to think that any of the methods of reasoning we use for descriptive claims can apply to them.

The *law of excluded middle* (every claim is true or false) and the *law of non-contradiction* (no claim is both true and false) are called "laws" by some because they lie at the heart of their metaphysics. But we can just as well see them as rules to simplify our reasoning. Or we can see them as reflecting a human capacity or need to classify as either-or. No matter. Let's assume them now. By agreeing to view prescriptive sentences as true or false but not both in the particular context in which they are used, we will be able to use many of our usual rules for reasoning. We'll return to this point here and in the essays that follow.

Let's be explicit about what we take to be true or false in our reasoning.

Claims   A claim is a written or uttered part of language that we agree to view as being either true or false but not both.

Some say that claims are only representatives of the things that really are true or false, such as thoughts or abstract propositions. Those people, though, use ordinary declarative sentences when reasoning with other people. So in our discussions we can focus on these linguistic objects, relating them as necessary later to further metaphysical assumptions about what is true or false.

By "agreement" here I do not mean there has to be a conscious, explicit statement that we will view the sentence as a claim, though there may be. Often agreements are manifested in lack of disagreement and in our reasoning together. Agreements may be due to physiological, psychological, or perhaps metaphysical reasons. All we need is that we can recognize when we are treating a sentence as having a truth-value.

3. The metaphysical basis of truth

We take certain descriptive claims as basic. We accept them or reject them on the basis of standards that do not depend on reasoning. For example, "I feel cold," "This is a rock," "What is red is not white." There are very different stories about why we are justified in believing such claims: empiricism, idealism, platonism, nominalism, ... We might say that "The earth revolves around the sun" and "Richard L. Epstein lives in New Mexico" are true if and only if they describe how the world is, but that conceals the metaphysics we take as the grounds for each to be true.

Any logical analysis, any story of how to reason well, whether with descriptive claims or, as we shall see, with prescriptive claims, will eventually end in a metaphysics. At that point the logician hands over the task of analyzing the nature of the evaluation of claims to the metaphysician. The job of the logician is to develop methods of reasoning that are compatible with a wide range of metaphysics or to develop different systems that reflect different underlying metaphysics. What I shall try to do here is give an analysis that will be suitable for a wide range of assumptions about why certain prescriptive claims are true or false. Perhaps a further study of the differences in the metaphysical bases will lead to a variety of systems.

4. Plausibility

Example 3   Dick, Zoe, Maria, Suzy, and Manuel are in Dick and Zoe's kitchen. It's cold outside, and there's a light breeze blowing in the window. They're having a good conversation and don't want to break it up, and there's no place else in their home to continue.

Dick: I'm cold, cold enough that my back is starting to cramp up.
Zoe: You should close the window.
Manuel: You should go for a walk. It'll take your mind off it.

Analysis Whatever we think of prescriptive claims, we can all agree that Zoe's advice is better than Manuel's.

We agree to view a claim that is good advice as true and one that is bad advice as false. But we naturally grade advice on a scale from very bad to very good. This seems to be in contrast to our usual notion of truth for descriptive claims: truth and falsity are a dichotomy. A claim is true or false, not sort of true, or a little false. It seems we need a notion of truth and falsity that is susceptible to grading by degrees.

But for descriptive claims we also have a scale.

Plausible claims A *claim is plausible* if we have good reason to believe it. It is less plausible the less reason we have to believe it. A claim that is not plausible is *implausible* or *dubious*.

The classification of claims as plausible or implausible is on a scale from the most plausible—ones we recognize as true—to the least plausible—those we recognize as false. Though we do not have precise measures of plausibility, we can often compare the plausibility of claims, and by being explicit about our background we can usually agree on whether we will take any particular claim to be plausible.[2] If we did not think that we can share our judgments of which claims are plausible, we would have no motive for trying to reason together. So if I say a claim is plausible without specifying a particular person or context, I mean it's plausible to most of us now as I'm writing.

Some people have devised systems for reasoning with descriptive claims that recognize degrees of truth in terms of plausibility or other notions. They have argued that truth and falsity is not a dichotomy. Nonetheless, in each of those systems a dichotomy is imposed on claims. A line is drawn that says on this side are claims that have designated truth-value: they are the ones we can use to derive further claims; on the other side are the claims with undesignated truth-value. In all our reasoning, no matter how much we deny it, we impose a dichotomy on claims—the true-false division—with other aspects of claims, for instance their plausibility, factored in as additional content.[3] So let's begin by recognizing only a true/good advice vs. false/bad advice dichotomy, leaving to later any attempt to factor degrees of acceptability into our evaluations.

5. Bad advice is false

With our dichotomy of the true and false we have to ask whether certain sentences that appear to be claims but are stupid, or senseless, or bad, or worthless (depending on the particular notions we are investigating) should be classified as claims. For example:

> If the moon is made of green cheese, then 2 + 2 = 4.
>
> The King of France is bald.
>
> Green dreams jump peacefully.

The last is a declarative sentence, but it doesn't make sense. We can envision no context in which we would want to reason with it. We say it is not a claim.

The other two, however, can show up in our reasoning. It may be a simplification to call them true or false rather than senseless or stupid, but if so it is a simplification of considerable utility. So we classify them as claims. But not as true claims. They are false because they are not suitable to proceed on for deducing true claims. In almost all systems of reasoning we take falsity as the default truth-value. A claim must pass certain tests in order to be true; all others are classified as false.[4]

There is, then, nothing unusual in our classifying advice that is stupid, or worthless, or nonsense, or perhaps just trivial as false. That there may be sentences we find difficult to classify because they are in some sense on the borderline does not mean the division is not suitable in cases where it is clear.

Example 4 Dick has been hiccuping for over three hours. He's going crazy with it. He's desperate. Suzy says to him, "You should hold your breath for four minutes. That will cure your hiccups for sure."

Analysis Dick can't hold his breath for four minutes. No one can. It's not possible. This is stupid advice. So "You should hold your breath for four minutes" is false.

Example 5 (Continuing Example 3)
> Manuel: No, no, no. You ought to start shivering. That's the best way for you to warm up.

Dick feels so cold that he's on the verge of shivering when Manuel makes his suggestion. Immediately he starts shivering.

Analysis We can't say that Dick followed Manuel's advice because it wasn't possible for him not to do what Manuel suggested. Manuel's advice is worthless, no better than saying "You should digest your food" or "You should let the sun rise tomorrow morning." Worthless advice is bad. So Manuel's claim is false.

By agreeing to classify worthless, bad, or senseless advice as false, we have found two conditions a prescriptive claim must satisfy for it to be true:

- It must be possible to do what is prescribed.
- It must be possible not to do what is prescribed.

But what exactly does it mean to say that it's possible to do what is prescribed?

6. Possibilities

A possibility is a way the world could be, however you construe that. To invoke a way the world could be when we wish to reason together we have no choice but to use a description. A description of the world is a collection of claims: we suppose that this, and that, and this are true. We do not require that we give a complete description of the world, for no one is capable of presenting such a description or of understanding one if presented. All we need are collections of claims to serve as our descriptions of how the world could be.

But not any collection of claims will do. Since the collection is meant to be a description of how the world could be, and no claim is both true and false, we cannot have both a claim and a contradictory of it in the collection. Further, any consequence of the claims in the collection also has to be reckoned to be part of the description, for otherwise we could have a contradiction. So if a way the world could be is that Ralph is a bachelor, then Ralph is a man is also part of that description.

A prescription, however, doesn't say how the world is, but how it should be. So the possibilities for it are relative to how the world actually is.

Example 6 Richard L. Epstein should resign from being President of the United States.

Analysis It's not possible for me to resign from being President given the way the world is now, since I'm not President.

Example 7   (Zoe to Dick) You should have taken Spot for a walk last night.

Analysis   We reason not only about what should be but what should have been. To evaluate this example we have to know whether it was possible for Dick to have taken Spot for a walk last night. The possibilities that matter for a prescriptive claim are those relative to how the world is or was at the time the prescription is meant to apply.

Example 8   Dick should graduate high school.

Analysis   Dick already graduated high school. And you can only graduate high school once. So it's not possible, relative to the way things are now, for Dick to graduate high school.

Example 9   Dick should be seated.

Analysis   Though Dick is already seated, this prescription is not worthless. He could get up. Or he could remain seated. Both are possibilities relative to the way the world is.

Example 10   Dick should go to Florida by flapping his arms like wings.

Analysis   It's not *physically possible* for Dick to fly that way. What we count as a possibility for a prescription is what can be done.

Example 11   (Continuing Example 3)
Dick should close the window.

Analysis   We count it as possible for Dick to close the window even if the window is stuck so badly that it would take tools and lots of effort to close it. What's physically possible isn't what is necessarily easy or obvious to do.

Example 12   (Continuing Example 3)
Dick should close the window.

Analysis   We wouldn't say that Dick followed this prescription if he closed the window the next day. A prescription is to do now what's prescribed. That Dick will be dead eighty years from now doesn't count as a possibility in evaluating this claim.

What counts as "now" is often only implicit. Sometimes it's within the next 10 minutes; sometimes it's within the next day; sometimes it's within the next year; and sometimes we have only a vague idea of the "due date" for a prescription. Unless we can clarify how long the *now* of a prescription lasts—by questioning, by give and take, by coming to an agreement—the sentence is too vague to be taken as a claim. In the examples below I'll assume it's (more or less) clear what the "now" of the prescription is meant to be.

The possibilities that matter in evaluating prescriptive claims are those that are *physically possible given the way the world is at the time the prescription is meant to apply.* For short, I'll say *given the circumstances* or *given what's true* at that time. This amounts to indexing prescriptive claims with the time the prescription is meant to apply. In what follows I'll assume that's clear even if it's only implicit.

7. Inferences and arguments

In our reasoning we're often concerned not only with whether a claim is true or is false but whether it follows from some other claims.

Inferences An *inference* is a collection of claims, one of which is designated the **conclusion** and the others the **premises**, which is intended by the person who sets it out either to show that the conclusion follows from the premises or to investigate whether that is the case.

There are various uses of inferences in reasoning: arguments, explanations, mathematical proofs, conditional inferences, and causal inferences are all examined in this series of books. What counts as a good/acceptable inference depends on which kind we're evaluating. Central to all those evaluations are the following notions.

Valid, strong, and weak inferences An inference is *valid* if it is impossible for the premises to be true and conclusion false at the same time and in the same way.

An inference is *strong* if it is possible but unlikely for the premises to be true and conclusion false at the same time and in the same way. An inference is *weak* if it is neither valid nor strong.

The classification of invalid inferences is on a scale from strongest to weakest as we deem more or less likely the possibilities we consider in which the premises are true and conclusion false.

For reasoning with descriptive claims we have both a theoretical and practical basis for evaluating inferences as valid, strong, or weak, as explained in "Arguments" in *The Fundamentals of Argument Analysis* and illustrated with hundreds of examples in *Critical Thinking*. In Section B we'll look at how these notions apply to inferences in which prescriptive claims appear.

One kind of inference is important in reasoning to truths.

Arguments   An *argument* is an inference that is intended by the person who sets it out to convince someone (possibly himself or herself) that the conclusion is true.

An argument is good if it gives good reason to believe the conclusion. The following conditions are necessary for that.

Necessary conditions for an argument to be good
- The premises are plausible.
- The argument does not *beg the question*:
  each premise is more plausible than the conclusion.
- The argument is valid or strong.

These conditions are relative to a particular person, though we can have confidence that they establish a shared standard for the evaluation of arguments involving only descriptive claims. Whether they are also sufficient is a large topic, which is examined in *The Fundamentals of Argument Analysis*. In what follows, though, I'll generally treat them as both necessary and sufficient.

Arguments are meant to lead to belief, and with that goes a standard of rationality: it's irrational to accept that an argument is good and not believe its conclusion. For prescriptions, though, it's not only belief but actions that matter for rationality.

Example 13   (Continuing Example 2)
    Physician: You shouldn't smoke anymore.
    Matilda: I agree.
Matilda leaves the physician's office and lights up a cigarette and continues to smoke cigarettes for the next week.

Analysis   The example describes a way the world could be: a person believes a "should"-claim but acts in contradiction to it. Just because you should do something, even if you believe you should do it, doesn't mean you actually do it. But if you don't, you're irrational.

The mark of irrationality for prescriptions   A person is irrational to believe a prescription and to act consciously in a way that he or she knows is incompatible with it.

Example 14   Wanda believes "You should not harm dogs," yet she gives her new puppy a square of chocolate every day.

   Analysis   Wanda isn't acting irrationally. She doesn't realize that giving her puppy a square of chocolate every day is incompatible with not harming dogs.

   We need to be clearer about what we mean when we say that acting in a particular manner is incompatible with a prescription. To begin, let's examine the simplest kind of prescription.

8. Simple "should"-claims

Simple "should"-claims   "You should do X" is a general form of a simple "should"-claim, where:

   "you" refers to a particular person to whom the claim is addressed,

   "do X" is a label for a blank that can be filled with a verb phrase.

   Thus, "do X" could be "close the window," or "put on a sweater," or "kill this vicious cat." I'll use roman capitals X, Y, Z for verb phrases or grammatical variations in what follows. I'll also use those letters to stand for descriptions of actions, such as "closing the window" or "barking at a cat" or "meows piteously." So when I talk about an action X, I mean for X to stand for a description. I'll trust that by context it will be clear which use of these is meant.

9. Consistency of actions and prescriptions
We can use our ordinary notion of consistency for descriptive claims to clarify what it means for two actions to be inconsistent or for a prescription and an action to be inconsistent. We begin with a definition.

Converting prescriptions and descriptions of actions into descriptive claims
Given a description of an action X done or to be done by a particular person, the ***descriptive claim associated with*** X, A_X, is a claim that

describes the world in which that person does X and which says no more than that: "That person does X."

Given a prescriptive claim "You should do X," the *associated descriptive claim* is A_X : "You do X."

For example, the conversion of "barking at a cat by Spot" is "Spot barks at a cat." The conversion of "Dick should close the window" is "Dick closes the window." There might not be a unique claim to serve as a conversion of a description of an action or a prescription, but there seems to be no point in trying to be more precise than to say that the conversion describes the world in which the action is done and says no more than that. The last clause is important. We don't take "Spot barks at a cat loudly until midnight" as a conversion of "barking at a cat by Spot."

Now we can clarify what we mean by saying it's possible to do a prescription.

Possibility of doing an action   Given a prescription "You should do X" where "you" refers to a particular person:

It is possible to do X means: It is possible for A_X to be true.

It is possible not to do X means: It is possible for not-A_X to be true.

Remember that when we say it's possible for A_X to be true we mean it's physically possible given the way the world is at the time the prescription is meant to apply.

Now we can say what we mean for a prescription and an action to be incompatible.

Compatibility of an action with an action or a prescription

An action X and an action Y are *compatible* or *consistent* if the associated claims A_X and A_Y are consistent. They are *incompatible* or *inconsistent* if A_X and A_Y are not consistent.

A prescription "You should do X," where "you" refers to a particular person, and an action Y done or to be done by that person are *compatible* or *consistent* if the associated claims A_X and A_Y are consistent. They are *incompatible* or *inconsistent* if A_X and A_Y are not consistent.

So "Matilda should stop smoking" and Matilda smoking a cigarette are inconsistent because "Matilda stops smoking" and "Matilda smokes a cigarette" are inconsistent according to our usual notion of consistency for descriptive claims. The conversion of descriptions of actions to descriptive claims allows us to clarify the notion of a consequence of an action or of a prescription.

An action or a prescription implies an action   An action X or a prescription "You should do X" (*likely*) *implies* an action Y if the inference "A_X therefore A_Y" is valid (strong). In that case we say that Y *is a* (*likely*) *consequence* of X or of "You should do X."

Now let's consider prescriptions that aren't simple.

10. "Shouldn't"
We not only prescribe what should be done, we often say what shouldn't be done.

Example 15   (Continuing Example 3)

Dick: I'm cold, cold enough that my back is starting to cramp up.
Zoe: You should close the window.
Maria: No, you shouldn't.

Analysis   There are two ways we can understand what Maria said:

(a) Not: You should close the window.

(b) You should refrain from closing the window.

These are not equivalent: (a) could be true because it's impossible to close the window, while for (b) to be true it must be possible to close the window. The first could be true, and Dick believes it, yet it would not be inconsistent for him to close the window: all it says is that closing the window isn't something he should do. The second says he should not do it, so that if he believes it and closes the window, he is irrational. The latter is advice; the former is not advice but the negation of advice.

You might say that the first is really a negation, too: "Refrain from closing the window" means "Do not close the window," which is a negation. But Maria could have said "You should leave the window open," in which case "You should close the window " is the "negation" of the action. It's simpler and clearer to think of refraining from doing something as just another way of acting. But what's refraining?

Right now there's a lot I'm not doing: I'm not eating, I'm not sleeping, I'm not jumping out of a plane without a parachute, I'm not jumping out of a plane with a parachute, ... The list is endless. But there are only a few things I am refraining from doing: scratching my head, looking out the window, sitting up straighter in my chair. At the very least, it seems that to refrain from doing something you have to be aware that you could do it. Whether refraining also requires a conscious choice about what to do is an issue we'll return to later.

"Shouldn't"   Given a claim "You shouldn't do X" we can interpret it as either of:
- It's not the case that you should do X.
- You should refrain from doing X.

Which of these readings is intended is often clear from context. When it isn't, we have to choose one in order to treat the sentence as a claim.

11. General "should"-claims
Often when we say "You should do X" we mean it not for one particular person but for everybody.

Example 16   Dick (to Zeke): You should never mistreat a dog.

Analysis   When Dick said this he meant it to apply not just to Zeke but as a general prescription applying to everyone.

When the "you" in "You should do X" is meant as "everyone in every context," it seems that there is an obvious, single way to analyze the claim according to the usual way we deal with quantifications.

General "should" claims
G   "You should do X" meant to apply to all people and all times is true if and only if "For any person in any context, that person should do X" is true.

But on the second understanding of "should"-claims presented in Section C we'll see that this is ambiguous.

12. Impersonal "should"-claims

Prescriptive claims in the passive or impersonal voice sound authoritative. But that's because they don't specify clearly to whom the prescription is made.

Example 17 One should always obey the law.

Analysis This sounds impersonal, but it's a general "should"-claim.

Example 18 Cigarettes should be taxed more heavily in this state.

Analysis It's the legislature and governor who are the only ones who can do this, so we can understand the claim as directed to them.

Example 19 There should be a law against drunken drivers.

Analysis Again, this is a prescription for the legislature and governor. That there already is a law against drunken drivers doesn't make it false since it's possible, given the circumstances, for there not to be one in the future.

Example 20 Society should ensure that everyone has the necessities: a good place to sleep, food, clothing, and a chance to do productive work.

Analysis This appears to be addressed not to any one person but to all people in our society as a collective. It can't be meant to apply to legislators since electing the right legislators is part of the "should." It is only we collectively who can do the action.

But to say that something should be done collectively is an unclear way of saying that all of us should individually do something, either working together or not. The claim is best understood as:

Each of us should do what we can towards ensuring that everyone in our society has the necessities: a good place to sleep, food, clothing, and a chance to do productive work.

Example 21 We should go to war against Iran.

Analysis We could read this as we did the last one: each of us should do what we can to ensure that we go to war against Iran. Or we can read it as we did Example 18: the government should take us into a war with Iran. It would be a mistake, however, to read it as a general claim prescribing that each of us should take up arms and fight against Iran, for that would be trading on the ambiguity of "go to war."

In some cases, though, there's seems to be no one person or people to whom the claim is meant to be addressed.

Example 22   The surgeon is getting ready to cut open the patient to take out his appendix. She's paying close attention to the patient and cannot take her eyes off him, and she's so focused she doesn't note who else is in the operating room.

> Surgeon: The anesthetic should be administered now.

Analysis   We can view this as addressed implicitly to whoever is in the room who can administer the anesthetic. But what if there is no one in the room who can do that? The claim could still be true: it should be administered by someone. It seems that the claim should be understood as:

> Someone should administer the anesthetic now.

We can understand this as meaning:

> There is a person and that person should administer the anesthetic.

But what if the surgeon is operating in some remote impoverished country where there isn't anyone within one hundred kilometers who knows how to administer anesthetic? The surgeon might know that and still make the claim: there's no one, but there should be someone. The correct reading of her claim is:

> There should be someone who can administer the anesthetic now, and that person should administer the anesthetic now.

But what kind of claim is "There should be someone who can administer the anesthetic now"? That sounds more like a wish than a claim: "Would that the world were different." There is no prescription to anyone to do anything.

Nonetheless the surgeon, if asked, would say that she believes it. In that case, there are a couple readings we could make. One is to see it as a conditional:

> If this hospital/country were organized to a minimally adequate standard for health purposes, then there should be someone who can administer the anesthetic now.

But that sounds odd: rather than "should," we expect "would," and then the claim is a descriptive counterfactual.

Alternatively, we could see it as a prescription to all people who run/organize health services in the country: "You should make available someone now who can administer the anesthetic." But that claim is false because it isn't possible to do what's prescribed: they can't do it immediately. Yet the surgeon wouldn't accept that she has said something that is trivially false. Nor could the claim be understood as a prescription to do something in the future because the surgeon means it when she says "now." Perhaps, if the surgeon knows that there's no one who can administer the anesthetic, we could construe the example as a past-tense prescription:

> There should have been someone who could administer the anesthetic now.

Generally, though, it seems that when a sentence using "should" looks like a prescription to do what can't be done in the sense of prescribing that the world be changed so that it could be done, the sentence is better understood as a wish than as a claim.

Example 23   Dick: The Governor should sign legislation outlawing cock fighting.

Zoe: But the legislature hasn't passed any legislation like that.

Analysis   We can say that the claim Dick makes is false because it's not possible for the Governor to do that. Or we can see Dick's claim as a counterfactual conditional: "Were there legislation outlawing cock fighting, then the Governor should sign it."

Example 24   Harry has been studying biology, evolution, and ecology. He's studying a particular area near town and says:

> There should be more species of birds here.

Analysis   This sentence is not a prescription. Rather, it can be understood as stating what current theories of evolution or theories of what a healthy ecosystem might suggest. The "should" is a variation on "it's most likely that" as in "it's predicted that," which is not the "should" of prescriptions.

Example 25   Dick: There should be no cats.

Analysis   This seems like a wish. But Dick believes the sentence, for it is a tenet of the Church of Dog. In that case perhaps we could read it as a descriptive claim: "The world would be a better place were there no cats." Though Dick agrees with that, he says it's not the correct reading of the sentence, for he takes it as a commandment of Dog, a real prescription. In that case it is a prescription to all (who believe) that they should do what they can to rid the world of cats.

13. Second-order prescriptions

Sometimes a prescription is to do other prescriptions.

Example 26   Zoe (to Dick): You should follow your doctor's advice.

Analysis   What Zoe says amounts to "You should do what your doctor says you should do." This is a "should"-claim whose advice is to do a range of actions. Suppose the doctor has told Dick that he should give up smoking cigars, that he should get more exercise, that he should get at least eight hours of sleep every night, and that he should drink only in moderation. It would seem, then, that Zoe's claim is equivalent to the following:

> You should give up smoking cigars, and you should get more exercise, and you should get at least eight hours of sleep every night, and you should drink only in moderation.

But we'll see on the second approach to reasoning with prescriptive claims in Section C that this reading can be ambiguous.

Example 27   You should kill all rabid dogs.

Analysis   It's not possible for me, or you, or anyone to kill all rabid dogs: there are rabid dogs throughout the world and no one can be everywhere and have the ability to do such killing were he or she there. We have to understand "You should kill all rabid dogs" as "You should kill all rabid dogs you can." Here "you" is meant as "everyone."

The more difficult question is how to understand the other quantification. We might consider the claim to be a prescription to do one thing: kill all rabid dogs.

> You should: for all x (if x is a rabid dog you can kill, kill x).

That is, what you should do is:

> For all x (if x is a rabid dog you can kill, kill x).

That reading is odd and would require us to develop some method of reasoning with quantifications within prescriptions.

More natural is for us to view it as a summing up of many prescriptions like: "You should kill Horatio," "You should kill Nefertiti," and . . . . Since we can't name all rabid dogs, we use a quantifier instead, reading the example as a prescription to do a range of actions:

> For all x (if x is a rabid dog you can kill, then you should kill x).

14. Value judgments as prescriptions
Value words like "good," "bad," "right," "wrong," and many others are often used to make prescriptions.

Example 28   Dick has just given his dog Spot his daily meal. He sees Flo, who's six years old, approaching Spot.

    Dick: It's best not to try to play with Spot when he's eating.

    Analysis   This appears to be a value judgment. But it's a prescription. We should understand it as "You shouldn't try to play with Spot when he's eating" in the reading of refraining.

Example 29   Dick: Eating dogs is bad.

    Analysis   This looks like a value judgment. But it's also a prescription. We should understand it as "You shouldn't eat dogs."

15. Other ways to make prescriptions
There are many other ways we make prescriptions. Compare:

    You should close the window

    You are required to close the window.

    You ought to close the window.

    You have to close the window.

    You need to close the window.

    You must close the window.

    You are obliged to close the window.

The differences among these amount only to a matter of the emphasis we give to our advice. "You must close the window" is "You should close the window" with an indication of the urging being closer to a command than advice. We might say, though, that "required" means "should" with regard to a rule or law.

    Closely related to such prescriptions are claims that do not offer advice but rather permission:

    You are allowed to close the window.

    You may close the window.

    You are permitted to close the window.

The differences here are also only a matter of emphasis, though we might say that "permitted" means that the permission is given with regard to a rule or law. Though none of these is prescriptive in the sense of prescribing some action, they can be understood in relation to "should"-claims. For example, "You are allowed to close the window" can be understood as "It's not the case that you should refrain from closing the window."

"Allowed"-claims   "You are allowed to do X" will be analyzed as "It is not the case that you should refrain from doing X."

We don't need to say that the two sentences mean the same, but only that we (agree that) can use the latter in place of the former in our reasoning.

Prohibitions, too, can be understood in relation to "should"-claims. "You are prohibited from closing the window" can be taken to be equivalent to "You should refrain from closing the window."

"Prohibited"-claims   "You are prohibited from doing X" will be analyzed as "You should refrain from doing X."

So "You are not prohibited from doing X" can be replaced in our reasoning by "You are allowed to do X."

16. Complex prescriptive claims

We can combine prescriptive claims with other prescriptive claims or with descriptive claims to form complex claims, as when Zoe said, "If Dick doesn't do the dishes after dinner tonight, he should walk Spot." We can also use quantifications with prescriptive claims, as we saw in Example 27. We call a prescriptive (or descriptive) claim *atomic* if it has no linguistic structure that we agree to take into account in our reasoning. Thus, "Dick should close the window" is atomic, as are all simple "should"-claims.

To extend an analysis of truth-conditions to complex prescriptive claims we can use any method of reasoning, formal or informal, which we usually employ for descriptive claims so long as the assumptions of that method (logic) do not contradict the assumptions we make in our understandings of atomic prescriptive claims.

This concludes the general background for prescriptive claims that we'll use in what follows.

B. Standards for Prescriptive Claims

Often we justify a prescriptive claim by invoking a standard from which it follows.

1. Examples of standards

Example 30   Dick: We shouldn't leave the lights on when we're away.
Zoe: Why?
Dick: Because we should do all we can to conserve energy.

Analysis   Dick justifies his "should"-claim by invoking another "should"-claim from which his follows.

Example 31   The Federal Reserve Board should lower interest rates.

Analysis   When Zoe said this, her mother disagreed because she wants to see her savings earn more interest. Zoe says that's the wrong standard. She's assuming "The Federal Reserve Board should help the economy grow, and lowering interest rates will help the economy grow," from which her claim would follow.

Example 32   Smoking destroys people's health. So we should raise the tax on cigarettes.

Analysis   Something's missing in this argument. Why should smoking being bad for the health of people lead us to believe that we should raise the tax on cigarettes? We need a claim like "We should tax activities that are destructive of people's health." But then why should we believe this? When we ask that, we're asking for a more fundamental prescriptive claim as a standard.

Example 33   It's wrong to murder people.

Analysis   This might seem as fundamental a prescriptive claim as we can find. But the qualifications people give suggest that we normally evaluate it against some more fundamental standard, even though we have difficulty enunciating that.

This method of justifying a prescriptive claim in terms of it following from other, more fundamental prescriptive claims can be taken as a general principle.

Prescriptive claims and standards
>   **PS**   Every prescriptive claim either states a standard or assumes/requires another prescriptive claim as standard.

To use this principle we need to be clearer about (i) how we evaluate whether an inference involving prescriptive claims is valid, strong, or weak, and (ii) what counts as a plausible or fundamental standard.

2. The Basic Rule of Consequence

In evaluating an inference that has a prescriptive premise, the possibilities we consider are those that describe what's physically possible given the way the world is at the time the prescription is meant to apply. That does not mean we need a full description of how the world is at that time. We take into account only as much of a description of the world as we need in our reasoning.

Example 34   (Continuing Example 3)
    Dick should close the window.
    Therefore, the window isn't closed.

Analysis   In any way in which the premise is true, it's possible to close the window. So the window isn't already closed. That is, given the circumstances, it's impossible for the premise to be true and conclusion false. The inference is valid.

Example 35   (Continuing Example 3)
    Dick should close the window.
    Therefore, the window isn't stuck.

Analysis   The premise could be true and conclusion false (see Example 11), so the inference isn't valid. To evaluate whether the inference is strong we need to know more about the situation.

A *prescriptive inference* is an inference from one or more prescriptive claims to a prescriptive claim.

Example 36   (Continuing Example 3)
    Dick should close the window.
    Therefore, Dick should get up out of his chair.

Analysis   Given what's true at the time of the prescription, it's not possible for Dick to close the window without getting out of his chair—where we understand the premise to mean that Dick should close the window himself and not just get Zoe to close it by complaining. Moreover, if the premise is true then it's possible for Dick to get out of his chair, for otherwise he couldn't close the window. And it's possible for Dick to remain seated, too. So any way in which the premise is true, the conclusion is true, too. The inference is valid.

Example 37 (Continuing Example 3)
　Dick should close the window.
　Therefore, Dick should put on gloves to grasp the top of the window and push down with more than 8 kg of force.
　Analysis This is not valid. If Dick does what's prescribed in the conclusion, he'll also do what's prescribed in the premise, but that's not the only way he can do what's prescribed in the premise. He could press down with bare hands and 6 kg of force, or he could pound the top of the window with a mallet, or . . . . It's possible for the premise to be true and conclusion false. The inference isn't even strong.

　In these last two examples we've evaluated a prescriptive inference by considering the inference that uses instead their associated descriptive claims. It seems that if the inference from A_X to A_Y is valid or strong, then the inference from "You should do X" to "You should do Y" is valid or strong. But there's an exception to that.

Example 38 Maria should attend her classes today.
　Therefore, Maria should breathe today.
　Analysis The inference from "Maria attends her classes today" to "Maria breathes" is valid or strong, given what's true at the time of the prescription. But that's because "Maria breathes" is true in every possibility we consider in evaluating the inference: it's not possible for Maria not to breathe. But that means the conclusion is false. Since the premise could be true, the inference is not only invalid, it's weak.

　Incorporating a clause to cover this last kind of example, we have the following rule.

A part of an action Doing Y is (*likely*) *a part of doing* X if:
- It's possible for A_Y to be false.
- "A_X therefore A_Y" is a (strong) valid inference.

The Basic Rule of Consequence for simple "should"-claims
If Y is (likely) a part of doing X, then the following inference is valid (strong):

　You should do X.
　Therefore, you should do Y.

Note that if A_Y is a consequence of A_X, then if it's possible to do X, it's also possible to do Y. And since doing Y is a part of doing X, it's also possible not to do Y.

This rule states a sufficient condition for a prescriptive inference to be valid or strong. Whether even for simple "should"-claims it is a necessary condition depends on what we mean by saying that a simple "should"-claim is true. All we can say now is that any such conception must be tested against this rule, either validating it or leading to a modification.

For the Basic Rule, as in all inference analysis, we allow that the premise(s) of the inference can be supplemented by other claims that are plausible to us and others.

Example 39   (Continuing Example 3)
Dick should close the window.
Therefore, Dick should take Spot for a walk later today.

Analysis   The premise, we can suppose, is true. The conclusion is true, too, but that's not because it follows from the premise. After all, "Dick closes the window, therefore Dick takes Spot for a walk" is weak. Hence the example is weak.

Example 40   (Continuing Example 30)
We should do all we can to conserve energy.
Therefore, we shouldn't leave the lights on when we're away.

Analysis   Dick and Zoe not leaving the lights on when they're away is likely a part of their doing all they can to conserve energy. So the conclusion follows: the inference is valid or strong.

Example 41   (Continuing Example 3)
Dick should close the window.
Therefore, Dick should make Maria unhappy.

Analysis   Maria really doesn't want the window closed: she's hot and that will make her hotter, and irritable, and plain unhappy. So "Maria is unhappy" is a consequence of "Dick closes the window" given the circumstances now. So the inference is valid. But that doesn't mean that Dick should make Maria unhappy. If, as we might think, "Dick should make Maria unhappy" is false, then since the inference is valid we can conclude that "Dick should close the window" is false.

Example 42 You should treat dogs as sacred. Ralph is a dog. Therefore, you should not torture Ralph.

Analysis This inference can be supplemented with the plausible claim "We should not torture that which is sacred." Then, as we can see by using the Basic Rule of Consequence, the inference is valid:

> You should treat dogs as sacred.
> Ralph is a dog.
>> Therefore, you should treat Ralph as sacred.

> We should not torture that which is sacred.
> You should treat Ralph as sacred.
>> Therefore, we should not torture Ralph.

Example 43 You should treat dogs as sacred. Ralph is a dog. Therefore, you should not kill Ralph.

Analysis This is not valid. It is possible for the premises to be true and conclusion false because "We sacrifice things we treat as sacred" is consistent with the premises.

Example 44 (Continuing Example 3)
> Dick should close the window.
> So Dick should not remain seated.

Analysis Given circumstances, "Dick closes the window" implies "Not: Dick remains seated" (see Example 36). So, it seems, we have by the Basic Rule "Dick should close the window" implies "Dick should not remain seated." That's correct, but we have to understand it in the sense of refraining from being seated.

Refraining as a consequence If not-Y is (likely) a part of doing X, then the following inference is valid (strong):

> You should do X.
> Therefore, you should refrain from doing Y.

---

3. Base prescriptive claims and general principles
We justify prescriptive claims on the basis of other prescriptive claims. Justification in this way is by arguments. To make an argument from, for example, "We should do all we can to conserve energy" to "We shouldn't leave the lights on when we're away," we need to be clear about how we judge the plausibility of prescriptive claims.

As with descriptive claims, we can ascribe plausibility to the conclusion of an argument according to the plausibility of the premises and the strength of the argument. However, that kind of justification can't go on forever.

Base prescriptive claims   A prescriptive claim is *base* if we intend/accept that no justification by reasoning can be given for it.

As we might take "This is a rock" to be a base descriptive claim, we might take "You should not torture children" as a base prescriptive claim. As there are different ways put forward for how to judge the truth or falsity of base descriptive claims, so, too, there are different ways put forward for how to judge the truth or falsity of base prescriptive claims.[5] As with descriptive claims, an investigation of those different ways is not the job of the logician. Our work is to set out how to reason compatible with a range of ways of evaluating base claims and to illuminate how those can be factored into our reasoning.

With prescriptive claims, at least in the examples above, it seems we look for more general claims from which to judge less general ones as plausible. Thus, "Zeke shouldn't torture Spot" follows from "We shouldn't torture dogs," which would have to be the more plausible claim on this approach.

With descriptive claims, we start with instances and then generalize. We then deduce instances of the generalization and accord plausibility to them because of such a deduction. But always, it seems, the general is deduced from more plausible particular claims.

Unless, that is, you happen to subscribe to a metaphysics that takes some very general descriptive claim as true with no instances cited as more plausible, for example "All is an illusion," "That which is true is that which I can perceive as such," "There are no universals," "The world is made up of things," "The world is process," . . . . All of us, when pushed far enough in trying to justify our belief in even the simplest claims, end up at such a place. Even in our daily reasoning, before we get to such metaphysical depths, we often have to invoke some general descriptive claim.

Example 45 Dick: Dogs are loyal. Dogs are friendly. Dogs can protect you from intruders. So dogs make great pets.

   Maria: Why does that follow?

   Analysis Maria's right. Dick's argument is missing some link from the premises—which he and Maria both accept as true—and the conclusion. Some general claim is needed, like "Anything that is loyal, friendly, and can protect you from intruders is a great pet." But that's exactly what Maria thinks is false: dogs need room to run around, they need to be walked every day, it costs more to take care of a dog than a goldfish. Just stating a lot of obvious truths doesn't get you the conclusion.[6]

Example 46   Zoe: We should go to Suzy's dinner party tonight.
   Dick: Why?
   Zoe: She invited us and she'll be very unhappy if we don't come.
   Dick: But I always have a miserable time at her dinner parties.
   Zoe: Look, we should go because she's our friend, and we
         shouldn't make our friends unhappy.

Analysis   Zoe is giving an argument for the conclusion "We should go to Suzy's dinner party tonight." We can analyze that as:

(1) Suzy is our friend.
(2) Suzy is giving a dinner party.
(3) Suzy will be unhappy if Dick does not go to her party.
(4) We shouldn't make our friends unhappy.
Therefore:
(5) We shouldn't make Suzy unhappy.
Therefore,
(6) Dick shouldn't make Suzy unhappy.
Assume:
(7) Dick does not go to the party.
Then:
(8) Suzy is unhappy.
Conclude: (6) and (8) are inconsistent.
Therefore, (7) is false.

Dick offers a counterargument, which we can fill in.

(a) Dick will have a miserable time if he goes to Suzy's party.
(b) Dick shouldn't do what makes him miserable.
Assume:
(c) Dick goes to Suzy's party.
Then:
(d) Dick will be miserable.
Conclude: (b) and (d) are inconsistent.
So (c) is false.

Dick and Zoe need to resolve who is right. That seems to depend on which of (4) and (b) is true, for we've seen they lead to incompatible prescriptions.

But Zoe says that Dick needn't accept (4). It's only (5) that he needs to accept. And there are good reasons for that:

Suzy is your friend.
She's always been good to you.
She'll really break down if you hurt her.
She'll be much more miserable if you hurt her than you will be
    if you go to her party.
Suzy is dumb as a post and gives lousy parties, but that's not
    because she isn't trying.
You don't want to live with my nagging about the misery
    you caused.
Tom, Suzy's boyfriend, will be really mad at you if you hurt
    her feelings.
Tom is your really good friend and you don't want to harm
    your friendship.

Dick agrees with all of these, but he still asks "So?" And just like Maria in the last example, he's right to do so. The obvious truths don't get Zoe her conclusion. A general claim is needed that will rule out other possibilities that might allow for the premises to be true and conclusion false.

It seems that when reasoning with prescriptive or descriptive claims we need to take some general principle as plausible without further justification in order to derive less general claims.

You might say that isn't so. The general claims we accept are generalizations from simpler, more basic claims. Yes, we have to accept some general principles that justify our making generalizations, but those are metalogical claims, different from the kinds we've been talking about. Flo, who's six years old, accepts "All dogs bark" because she's seen a lot of dogs and believes "Spot barks," "Ralph barks," "Juney barks," "Buddy barks," "Birta barks," "Anubis barks." Similarly, Zoe accepts the claim "We shouldn't make our friends unhappy" after considering enough examples like "I shouldn't make Suzy unhappy."

We're now at a divide that applies to descriptive as well as to prescriptive claims. Some say that we have some insight, some intuition that justifies our accepting certain general claims as true without invoking the truth of any of their instances. Those general principles are more plausible than any of their instances. Someone on the other side of the divide takes it that only the most particular simple claims can be justified without reason, and then we accept generalizations at some risk.[7] After all "All dogs bark" isn't true since there are basenjis that don't bark and some dogs with damaged or severed vocal cords can't bark. This view is most often invoked in modeling in the sciences. It is compatible with what we've done, as I discuss in "Prescriptive Theories?" in this volume.

4. Deciding between base prescriptive claims
The last example raised the question of how we can decide between base prescriptive claims.

Example 47   Dick: What are you doing?
     Dogcatcher: This dog just bit a child. I'm going to take it to the shelter and put it down.
     Dick: You shouldn't kill that dog.
     Manuel: Yes, you should kill it.
     Dogcatcher: Yes, I should kill it.

Analysis   Dick means his claim to be judged relative to the standard "You should never kill a dog," where "you" is meant to be all people. Clearly his claim follows from that. But why should Manuel and the dogcatcher accept that standard?

Dick offers a more fundamental claim "You should treat dogs as sacred" along with the descriptive claim "When you (intentionally) kill a creature, you are not treating it as sacred."

(a) We should treat all dogs as sacred.
Therefore, you should treat this dog as sacred.
When you intentionally kill a creature, you are not treating it
    as sacred.
If you kill this dog, you will be doing it intentionally.
Therefore, if you kill this dog, you will not be treating it as sacred.
Therefore, if you treat this dog as sacred, you will not kill it.
Therefore, (from (a) and the Basic Rule for negations) you should
    not kill this dog (in the sense of refraining from killing).

Thus, "You shouldn't kill that dog" follows from Dick's standard along with other plausible descriptive claims. But Manuel and the dogcatcher disagree that "You should treat dogs as sacred" is true.

The dogcatcher thinks Dick is wrong. She takes as her standard "An employee of the city should do what he or she is paid to do, especially if it's a rule or law of the city."

> (b) An employee of the city should do what he or she is paid
>   to do, especially if it's a rule or law of the city.
> The dogcatcher is an employee of the city.
> Killing a dog that bit a child is part of what the dogcatcher is
>   paid to do, and it's a rule of the city.
> This dog bit a child in the city.
> Therefore, the dogcatcher should kill this dog.

This is a valid inference, and the descriptive claims that supplement the prescriptive one are plausible. Thus "You should kill this dog" follows from her standard.

So who is correct? Each eventually works back to what he or she considers a base prescriptive claim, one for which they consider no further claim is needed as justification. But they disagree about which of those is true.

How can we judge between different base prescriptive claims?

If we can see that one of the necessary conditions for a base prescriptive claim is false, such as that it's not possible to do what is prescribed, then we know that the claim is false. We can also say that if the base prescriptive claim has a consequence that is false or absurd, then it's false or unlikely to be true. To do so requires us to assume that any true prescription does not have a false consequence. But that is not enough. We also have to invoke the following.

Consistency is a fundamental principle   We should be consistent in our reasoning.

This is a base prescriptive claim we seem to invoke in all our reasoning. Our motive for accepting it is the same as why we require that no claim is both true and false.

Beyond considering the necessary conditions for a base prescriptive claim to be true, and invoking consistency as a necessary condition, we can only invoke whatever method or criteria we have for determining the truth or falsity of a base prescriptive claim as our justification of why a base prescriptive claim is true or possible. In Example 46, Dick and Zoe must reflect on whatever methods they have of determining the truth or falsity of base prescriptive claims to find a way out of their disagreement.

Sometimes, though, the question isn't whether a particular base prescriptive claim is true or false, but what base claim is being invoked.

Example 48   Sarah: You should not eat dogs.

Dick: I agree.

Analysis   When Sarah said this to Dick, she meant it to apply not just to Dick but to everyone. When Dick agreed, did he know what standard Sarah had in mind?

Perhaps Sarah is a vegetarian and believes:

You should treat all animals humanely, and butchering animals is inhumane.

Given this, the example follows. Dick agrees with the prescriptive part, but he doesn't accept the descriptive claim that butchering animals is inhumane.

Or perhaps Sarah believes:

Dogs taste bad and you shouldn't eat anything that tastes bad.

Given this, the claim follows, too. But Dick doesn't accept the descriptive part since he's never tasted dog meat.

Or perhaps Sarah believes:

We should not eat anything that is not kosher, and dog meat is not kosher.

Dick agrees with the descriptive part that dog meat is not kosher, but as he's of a different faith, he doesn't accept the prescriptive part. Eating lobster, which isn't kosher, isn't against his faith.

Or Sarah might just believe what many people do:

Dogs should be treated as companions to people and not as food.

Sarah had some standard in mind when she spoke, some other prescriptive claim from which the example follows.

Are we to say, then, that if Dick doesn't know what standard Sarah is invoking, he shouldn't view the example as a claim? No. Both agree that the sentence is a claim, though they may differ on not only the evidence they take for that, but on the grounds for the truth or falsity of it.

Dick agrees with Sarah, though he uses a different standard for why that claim is true. Dick believes that "Dogs should be treated as companions to people and not as food" is true, while, it turns out, Sarah believes "We should not eat anything that is not kosher, and dog meat is not kosher." These are not inconsistent. Indeed, none of the standards suggested above are inconsistent with any of the others.

When Dick is asked why he believes his claim, he might say it's because "Dog commands it so" is true. When Sarah is asked why she believes her claim, she might say it's because "God commands it so" is true. Neither can give a further justification; neither believes there is any need to do so. Their ultimate metaphysics of the prescriptive part of experience are different. But they agree on the truth-value of the example.

It is not necessary to know what standard is being invoked for us to take a prescriptive sentence as a claim.

5. "Ought" from "is"

a. Can an argument from prescriptive premises to a descriptive conclusion be good?
Example 34 is a valid inference whose only premise is prescriptive and whose conclusion is descriptive:

Dick should close the window.
Therefore, the window isn't closed.

You can't do what's already been done (it's not possible not to do it). More generally, both of the following are valid:

You should do X.
Therefore, it is possible to do X.

You should do X.
Therefore, X is not already done.

But no such inference is a good argument, for the premise is not more plausible than the conclusion.

It seems that any valid or strong argument with only prescriptive premises and a descriptive conclusion will be bad because it begs the question: at least one of the premises is not more plausible than the conclusion. But more investigation of this is needed, for I have no good analysis of why this has to be the case.

b. Can an argument from descriptive premises to a prescriptive conclusion be good?

One of the most discussed principles for prescriptive claims holds that the opposite kind of argument is never good.

You can't get "ought" from "is"

H   There is no good argument all of whose premises are descriptive and whose conclusion is prescriptive.

This has seemed obvious to many people. They say we can't conclude a way the world should be from knowing how the world is. Here's how David Hume justified it:

> I cannot forbear adding to these reasonings an observation, which may, perhaps, be found of some importance. In every system of morality, which I have hitherto met with, I have always remark'd, that the author proceeds for some time in the ordinary way of reasoning, and establishes the being of a God, or makes observations concerning human affairs; when of a sudden I am surpriz'd to find, that instead of the usual copulations of propositions, *is*, and *is not*, I meet with no proposition that is not connected with an *ought*, or an *ought not*. This change is imperceptible; but is, however, of the last consequence. For as this *ought*, or *ought not*, expresses some new relation or affirmation, 'tis necessary that it shou'd be observ'd and explain'd; and at the same time that a reason should be given for what seems altogether inconceivable, how this new relation can be a deduction from others, which are entirely different from it. But as authors do not commonly use this precaution, I shall presume to recommend it to the readers; and am persuaded, that this small attention wou'd subvert all the vulgar systems of morality, and let us see, that the distinction of vice and virtue is not founded merely on the relations of objects, nor is perceiv'd by reason.[8]

Hume seems to give the principle for valid inferences rather than the wider scope of good arguments. But it is (H) rather than Hume's formulation that is significant for reasoning with prescriptive claims.

We can dismiss one of Hume's reasons for accepting (H): any term that appears in the conclusion of an inference must appear in the premises for the inference to be valid (or, it would seem, strong). Though that condition is imposed throughout formal logics, it fails for many examples we encounter in our ordinary lives. For example,

Ralph is a bachelor.
Therefore, Ralph is not married.

This object is white all over.
Therefore, this object is not red.

Nonetheless, it might seem that by accepting our assumption that every prescriptive claim either states or depends on a prescriptive standard (PS, p. 23) we are committed to accepting principle (H). But nothing we have said so far precludes that the conditions for a base prescriptive claim to be true are entirely descriptive.

Naturalists say, roughly, that "good" and "bad," "just" and "unjust," and other moral terms can or should be defined in terms of "natural" predicates, that is, empirical ones. Those can be about the psychology of humans, or . . . . The metaphysicists, such as Kant, think that those notions can be defined in terms of descriptive metaphysical predicates. When only such predicates are used in a claim, the claim is descriptive.[9] So a claim of the sort "Killing cats is good" is reduced to or understood as a descriptive claim.

Whatever justification is given for that view can equally, it seems, be given for the view that "good advice" and "bad advice" can be defined in terms of descriptive claims. But if we take that what is good can be defined in terms of descriptive predicates, we are going to need a prescriptive claim in order to justify our acceptance of prescriptions.

You should do what's good   If (for you) to do X is good, then you should do X.

This is what we implicitly accepted when we said that value judgments are often meant as prescriptions.

However, the naturalist could say that no such additional claim is needed. The descriptive claims alone are what is meant by what should be done. And that view, which denies (H), is compatible with the approach to understanding prescriptive claims in terms of standards. It is, however, a view that is more natural in the second approach to reasoning with prescriptive claims which we'll see in Section C.

The opposite view, that no formulation of why a base prescriptive claim is true can be given in terms of descriptive claims, is also compatible with understanding prescriptive claims in terms of standards. One might cite intuition, insight, religious revelation, ...[10] If we take that view, then, it seems that principle (H) is correct. Some examples, though, suggest that it needs amendment. The first two are from A.N. Prior, and the third is a variation of one of his.[11]

Example 49 Tea-drinking is common in England. Therefore, either tea-drinking is common in England or all New Zealanders ought to be shot.

Analysis The premise is plausible and the inference is valid, assuming that you accept the logical principle: from A conclude A or B. But the premise is not more plausible than the conclusion, so the argument is not good.

Example 50 There is no man over 20 feet high. Therefore, there is no man over 20 feet high who is allowed to sit in an ordinary chair.

Analysis The premise is plausible and the inference is valid. But again, the premise is not more plausible than the conclusion, so the argument is not good.

Example 51 Sheriffs are employed by the state. Therefore, sheriffs ought to do whatever all people employed by the state ought to do.

Analysis Here the inference is valid and the premise is not only plausible but more plausible than the conclusion. This is a good argument.

These examples do not use the prescriptive claim in an essential way. In Example 49 any other claim could replace the part of the conclusion that is prescriptive and the inference would be just as good. In Example 50 the inference would be just as good if we replaced "is allowed to sit in an ordinary chair" with any other predicate. In Example 51 we can replace "ought to do" with any other predicate (suitably modifying the grammar) and get just as good an argument. We can modify (H) to eliminate counterexamples like these and get a principle that appears to be correct on a non-naturalistic standards approach to analyzing prescriptive claims.

A part of a claim does not appear essentially in an argument
A claim or a part of a claim *does not appear essentially* in an argument if all occurrences of it can be replaced by any other claim or or any other similar part of a claim yielding true claims for true claims and false claims for false ones and the argument is just as good.

H+ There is no good argument all of whose premises are descriptive and whose conclusion is prescriptive, where the prescriptive part of the conclusion appears essentially.

Example 52   Manuel: Let's invite Dick over to see the football game.
Maria: Dick promised to take Zoe to the movies today.
Manuel: So Dick should take Zoe to the movies today.

Analysis It appears that the last two claims constitute a good argument. The premise is plausible and more plausible than the conclusion. But the argument is not valid nor even strong. It might not be possible for Dick to take Zoe to the movies tonight, or Zoe might not want to go to the movies tonight, so Dick's promise is voided. Though a promise is the acceptance of an obligation, it is not itself an obligation: much must happen for it to be an obligation at the time for which the promise is to come into effect. What's missing to make the inference valid or strong is "One should (almost) always do what one has promised," which is prescriptive.

Example 53   Fischer wants to mate Botwinnik. The one and only way to mate Botwinnik is for Fischer to move his Queen. Therefore, Fischer ought to move the Queen.

Analysis Max Black argues that this is a valid inference in which the premises are descriptive and the conclusion is prescriptive.[12] Thus, we can derive "ought" from "is."

An analogous argument shows the flaw in Black's reasoning:

Dick wants to get drunk.
The one and only way to get drunk is to drink alcohol.
Therefore, Dick ought to drink alcohol.

Here it's obvious that a premise is missing:

Dick should do what he wants to do.

And more generally:

SW One should do what one wants to do.

This is wildly implausible—unless you're the kind of naturalist who thinks that satisfying desires is all there is to "ought." But then you're begging the question in claiming that this is true and hence that naturalism can't be demolished. The more common view is that SW is false.

Max Black recognizes that some premise is needed:

> It is often said that any argument of the above form is really an
> enthymeme with an unstated premise, possibly of the form:
>
>> Everybody should do anything which is the one and only
>> one way to achieve anything that he wants to achieve.
>
> Since this general premise is held to be "normative" or "practical,"
> its addition is held to convert the original inference into a formally
> correct one still conforming to [principle (H)]. My answer is that the
> proposed additional premise must be held to be analytic, in the sense
> of being guaranteed correct by virtue of the meanings or functions of
> the terms it contains. p. 173

But as we've seen, that premise isn't analytic; it isn't even true.

It might be said that for the example Max Black offers, a simpler
claim will do as an additional premise:

> In chess, one should do what one wants to do.

But even this doesn't seem right, as Fischer might not see that moving
the Queen is the best move and want to move the Knight instead.
Rather, we need something like:

> In chess, one should make the move that most likely will lead
> to checkmate.

That seems true, and given our background of understanding chess
we can treat the argument of this example as simply lacking a premise
to repair it, though not as an argument that violates principle (H$^+$).

C. Aims for Prescriptive Claims

In our daily life we often deem advice good if would lead to the
fulfillment of some aim.

1. Personal "should"-claims for a specified aim

Example 54 Dick has discovered some baby robins in a tree. He says
to Zoe, "You said you always wanted to see baby birds. So you should
go next door and look in that maple tree."

Analysis Dick first states that Zoe has a desire. Then he suggests
to Zoe a way to fulfill that desire. It seems that "should" here can be
construed as simply "will be able to fulfill your desire." "You should
go next door and look in the maple tree" is good advice because that's
a good way for Zoe to fulfill her desire to see baby birds.

Example 55   Maria isn't feeling well, and it's the day of a big exam in her chemistry course. She's desperate to pass that course.

> Dick (to Maria): You should go to school.
>
> Zoe: No, you shouldn't.

Analysis   Here "should" seems more imperative. But this example isn't so different from the previous one. It's just that here "desire" or "wish" are not quite right. Rather, "should" is being used like "will be able to accomplish your aims," and the aim here, though not stated explicitly, is for Maria to pass her course.

As Dick, Maria, and Zoe reason together, they will reason about what action will best fulfill Maria's aim. That's what Maria should do.

In these two examples the "should"-claim is directly addressed to the person who is being advised, and an aim that's meant to be fulfilled by the suggested action is either stated explicitly or is obvious though implicit. Let's look at just this kind of claim for now.

Personal "should"-claims for a specified aim

"You should do X in order to α" is the general form of a personal "should"-claim for a specified aim, where:

- "do X" is to be filled with a verb phrase;
- "α" is to be filled with an aim;
- "you" refers to a particular person to whom the claim is addressed.

I'll use Greek lower-case letters, α, β, . . . to stand for aims, such as "Never kill a dog" or "Get warmer," which are imperatives. Aims can also be phrased as infinitives. For example, if Dick asks Zoe why he should close the window, she might answer "In order to get warmer." I'll use "achieve" and "fulfill" indifferently in what follows.

Example 56   (Example 3 again)
Dick, Zoe, Maria, Suzy, and Manuel are in Dick and Zoe's kitchen. It's cold outside, and there's a light breeze blowing in the window. They're having a good conversation and don't want to break it up, and there's no place else in their home to continue.

> Dick: I'm cold, cold enough that my back is starting to cramp up.
>
> Zoe: You should close the window.

Analysis   Here Dick's aim is pretty clear: Get warm enough to stop his back cramps. Just as before, if the window can't be closed, then Zoe's advice is bad, only here that's more obvious: if it can't be done, it can't fulfill the aim. So suppose it's possible for Dick to close the window. Is Zoe's advice good?

If Dick needs it to be a lot warmer to get rid of his back cramps, and he needs that done soon, and closing the window will only make it a little warmer and will take awhile to do even that, then the advice isn't much better than doing nothing or searching for something else to do. Zoe's claim is bad advice/false.

On the other hand, if it's sunny despite a cool breeze, and the sun is shining strongly through the window so that closing the window is likely to warm up the room fairly quickly, we'd say that Zoe's claim is good advice/true. Dick should close the window. It will help him fulfill his aim.

Example 57   (continuing the previous example)

Dick: I'm cold, cold enough that my back is starting to cramp up.

Zoe: (a) You should close the window.

Maria: No, you should put on a sweater.

Dick: Why?

Maria: If you close the window, it'll be too stuffy and hot in here for me. Anyway, closing the window won't make it warmer in here very soon, while if you put on a sweater you'll stop being cold pretty quickly.

Analysis Maria's first comment denies (a) and offers another "should"-claim.

She explains why she thinks (a) is bad advice/false by asking Dick to consider an additional aim: don't make the room too stuffy and hot for her. Is that one of Dick's aims? Maria certainly hopes that by pointing it out it will be. If Dick follows the advice of (a), that is, if he closes the window, he can't fulfill this other aim.

But even if Dick doesn't adopt that aim, Maria offers a reason to prefer her advice to Zoe's. Doing what (a) prescribes isn't likely to fulfill Dick's aim very well, while following her advice Dick is more likely to achieve his aim.

Does that mean that Zoe's claim is false and Maria's is true? Certainly it means that Maria's advice is better than Zoe's. Perhaps we should assign relative values to advice. We could assign Maria's claim the value 7/8, and Zoe's claim 1/4. And if Dick and Zoe have a heating pad, we might assign the claim "You should get the heating pad and put it on your back" the value 1, the best advice. Advice that Dick take their dog Spot out for a walk in the cold without putting on a coat would get the value 0. Perhaps we don't want a simple dichotomy of true/false in evaluating "should"-claims in terms of aims but a scale on which we can rank them from bad to the very best. But assigning such values will not resolve which if either of Zoe's claim or Maria's claim is good advice/true. To do that we must draw a line, say at value .8, such that any claim that has a value greater than that is good advice/true, and all others are bad advice/false. So, as discussed in Section A.4, we still need to be clear first about what conditions count for advice to be good even if we assign a range of values to advice.

Example 58   Floyd and Betty are in the hallway in their high school. It's the first day of the school year, and Betty is a new student there.

Floyd: Gosh, you're over 6 feet tall. You should play basketball.

Betty: No way. I don't want to play basketball because you have to get all rough and smelly and it's not at all feminine.

Floyd: But if you play basketball, you could get a scholarship to college. And you'd help our team out. And you'd be using your height to an advantage.

Betty: So what? It's still rough and smelly and not feminine.

Analysis   Floyd says that Betty should play basketball in order to achieve specific aims. It seems that if Betty follows his advice, she'll be able to fulfill those aims. However, that doesn't make his advice good because Betty has another aim she values higher and that is incompatible with the aims that Floyd suggests. So the claim "You should play basketball" is bad advice/false.

We can clarify the idea that an aim and an action are incompatible in much the same way we did for prescriptions and actions.

Converting an aim to a descriptive claim   Given an aim α meant to be fulfilled by one or more persons, the ***descriptive claim associated with*** α, A_α, is a claim that describes the world in which that aim is achieved by that person or persons and says nothing more. An aim α is ***fulfilled*** if A_α is true

---

Again it's difficult to be precise, but I suspect that the conversion is usually straightforward: we convert an imperative such as "Do Y" or an infinitive such as "To do Y" into a claim "Y is done" or "Y happens" that describes the world in which the aim is done. In the context of a specified aim for a personal "should"-claim, we would take this to be "Y is done by you" where the reference for "you" is given.

Incompatibility of aims and actions An aim α and an action X are (*likely*) *incompatible* if A_α and A_X are (likely) inconsistent.

An aim α and an aim β are (*likely*) *incompatible* if A_α and A_β are (likely) inconsistent.

Two claims are more or less likely to be inconsistent according to whether we have a stronger or weaker argument for their inconsistency. Thus, Dick's aim "Get warmer" is incompatible with his taking a cold shower because "Dick is warmer" and "Dick takes a cold shower" are inconsistent, as we can show with a strong or valid argument. Similarly, Dick's aim "Kill any vicious cat you can" is incompatible with the aim Suzy hopes he has "Adopt this vicious cat and try to reform it" because "Dick kills this vicious cat" and "Dick adopts this vicious cat and tries to reform it" are inconsistent.

Now we can say that for "You should do X in order to α" to be good advice/true: (i) it has to be possible for the person to whom the claim is addressed to do X and possible not to do X; (ii) doing X should help to fulfill α; and (iii) that person has no other aim he or she values as highly which is incompatible with doing X. But what if doing X is only likely incompatible with some other aim the person holds as highly?

Example 59 Beth: You should let the sheep out to graze. They need more feed, and we're low on hay.

Sam: No. If I do, I might not be able to get them back into the corral before I have to leave for work.

Analysis Here the course of action that Beth suggests for Sam is only likely incompatible with an aim he considers more important than the aim Beth gives for her "should"-claim. I think most of us would say that Beth's advice in this case is bad/false. Holding an aim that is valued as highly as the aim behind the "should"-claim and that is likely incompatible with the course of action prescribed is enough to make the "should"-claim false.

We've classified a "should"-claim as good advice/true only if it seems likely that if the person does what's prescribed then the aim will be fulfilled. How likely does that have to be?

Example 60   Suzy: You should buy a lottery ticket. The prize is
$72 million.
        Zoe: That's stupid. There's almost no chance of winning.
        Suzy: But it's the only chance you have of getting rich.

   Analysis I think most of us would say that Suzy's "should"-claim
is bad advice/false. Yes, Zoe wants to be rich. But as Zoe points out,
there's little chance that following Suzy's advice would help her fulfill
her aim. The chance is negligible, only a tiny bit better than not
following the advice. It's better that Zoe keep her dollar.

Example 61   Dick and Tom are out in a row boat in the ocean fishing
three kilometers offshore. They decide to head back. They hit some
rocks. The impact knocks a hole in the boat and makes them drop their
oars. Their boat is filling up fast with water. The tide is going out.
The wind is getting up, and the sea is too cold and rough for them to
swim to shore. They see that the boat is filling with water faster than
they could bail. Nonetheless, Tom says, "You should start bailing."

   Analysis Even if Dick bails extraordinarily fast, he won't get
ahead of the rising water in the boat. They'll sink soon whether he
bails or doesn't bail; he can put off sinking only a little while. The
chance of Dick fulfilling his aim "Reach safety" by bailing is only
negligibly better than doing nothing. Yet it's his only chance of
fulfilling that aim.

   In this case, I think most of us would say that Tom's advice is
good/true. Though it only negligibly increases Dick's chance of fulfilling his aim, that's good enough in this situation because Dick values
that aim so highly and there's no better course of action he can see.[*]

   Whether a "should"-claim is good advice depends in part on how
much you want to achieve your goals, that is, how important your aim
is to you. Sometimes a negligible chance of fulfilling your aim is
enough to do something, sometimes it isn't.

   Whether a suggested action is the best way of achieving an aim
also depends on what other ways you could act.

Example 62   (continuing Example 57)
        Zoe: Actually, I think you should run down to the drugstore
              and buy a heating pad, then put it on your back.
        Dick: I don't have enough cash on me to do that.

* Dick and Tom were rescued by a passing sailboat filled with college
co-eds who were competing in a swimsuit modeling contest.

Zoe: You could stop at the bank first.

Dick: You're crazy—that's way too much trouble. Your first suggestion or Maria's is much better.

Analysis Dick reckons that Zoe's advice is bad/false. Yes, it would help him fulfill his aim of getting warmer, but it's too much trouble to do compared to the other options. It would also take too long, during which time his aim is not fulfilled. It isn't just whether the proposed action is likely to fulfill the aim, but how well it does that when compared to the other options, which takes into account time and ease of doing it.

Example 63 Father: You said you wanted to learn about ancient Greece. There's a trip to Greece for students planned by the university with a professor to see the ruins. You should go.

Beth: That sounds great. But I'm planning to spend the summer studying ancient Greek in an immersion course. I think that will be more helpful than just seeing ruins.

Father: But if you see the ruins and the countryside you'll have a better feel for the world the Greeks lived in.

Beth: I guess so, but not as much as if I learned their language and could read the plays and histories and philosophy they wrote.

Father: Maybe you could do both. Why not take the immersion course in the fall?

Analysis The claim at issue is "You should go to Greece on a trip with a professor to see the ruins." Beth and her father agree on her aim: to learn about ancient Greece. They differ on what is the best option for achieving that aim: studying Greek in an immersion course or going to Greece. These are incompatible courses of action.

From what's been said, it's difficult to judge which option is best. Partly that depends on how Beth absorbs new information and insight and how she responds to travel versus study. Her father suggests a third option: make the options compatible by taking the immersion course in the fall. Then Beth could do both.

When someone suggests "You should do X," one option we always consider is whether doing X is better than doing nothing at all. If, in the contexts we're considering, the people who are discussing the claim are aware of other options that might fulfill the aim, say Y and Z, then in evaluating whether the claim is good advice, they also need to consider doing any or all of the following:

Do nothing (refrain from doing X, Y, and Z).

Do X.

Do Y.

Do Z.

Do X and Y.

Do X and Z.

Do Y and Z.

Do X and Y and Z.

And similarly for more options.

Some of these might not be possible if the courses of action are incompatible. But often enough we choose to adopt more than one course of action if doing so is not too much work. In weighing whether a course of action is good, we consider not only how likely it is that doing it will help us achieve our aim(s) but also how difficult it is to do. That must be weighed against how much we want to achieve our aim(s).

For example, if Dick's back really hurts, he might close the window, put on a sweater, and apply a heating pad (Example 57). Does that mean that "You should close the window" is bad advice/false? No, it shows an ambiguity in "You should close the window." If it's meant as "You should close the window and nothing more," then it's bad advice/false. If it's meant as "You should at least close the window," then it's good advice/true. Usually we understand such claims to mean "at least" and not "only."

"Should" as "at least"   Unless context determines otherwise, we'll understand "You should do X" to mean "You should do *at least* X."

Example 64   Manuel: You should pull that goat-head weed out.
Zoe: Oh, it's small.
Manuel: But if you leave it there, it will take over your yard.
             You want to have a nice yard, don't you?

Analysis   Zoe indeed has the aim that Manuel specifies for his "should"-claim: to have a nice yard. Fulfilling that aim certainly requires not having a lot of weeds in the yard.

Doing what Manuel suggests will not fulfill Zoe's aim. That can only be done by weeding over many months, perhaps applying fertilizer, watering regularly, ... We might say that pulling the goat-head weed will further her aim, but that's not clear. What we can say, though, is that if Zoe doesn't pull the weed, then she will likely not be able to fulfill her aim or it will make it much more difficult to fulfill her aim. So following his advice is better than doing nothing; Manuel's "should"-claim is good advice/true.

Example 65   (Continuing Example 58)
>   Betty: Besides, I want to have children.
>   Floyd: Well, I can help you with that. You should come to my house this weekend—my parents will be gone.
>   Betty: You're crazy. I don't want to become a mother *now*.

Analysis   Betty has the aim to be a mother. Floyd says he can help her fulfill her aim. But Betty clarifies that her aim is for the future. What is preferable may not be the action that fulfills the aim soonest but one that fulfills it at the most propitious time.

What we aim for is in the future; if it were already achieved there would be no point in aiming for it except for it to continue, which is also in the future. Some of our aims are for the entire future, as when Manuel adopted the aim to live a morally good life. Other aims are for the immediate future, as when Dick wants to get warm. Others are for some time that's not clearly specified, as when Betty aims to be a mother. To evaluate a "should"-claim for a specified aim we need to know what time is meant as appropriate for the fulfillment of the aim. From now on let's assume that's either specified or we can infer it from context in what follows. When it's not clear, the sentence may be too vague to take as a claim.

Example 66   Suzy: You and Dick should stop arguing about his smoking cigars.
>   Zoe: Why?
>   Suzy: So you can stop your bickering about it.

Analysis   Suzy's advice is that Zoe should stop arguing in order to stop arguing. That's stupid. When Zoe asks "Why?", as anyone might to a "should"-claim, she expects a reason to follow the advice. The answer we expect is an aim: in order to . . . . It's circular to recast the advice as the aim which the advice is meant to fulfill. As before, we classify prescriptive claims that are senseless, stupid, etc. as bad advice and, hence, false.

2. Fulfilling aims

What does it mean to say that "You close the window" leads Dick closer to fulfilling his aim of getting warmer? It's tempting to think in terms of probabilities: there is a higher probability of Dick being warmer given that he closes the window than if he does nothing. But to invoke probabilities would require us to give a numerical analysis where there is no obvious or even non-arbitrary way to assign probabilities to the claims involved.

In any case, a probability analysis would be an unclear shorthand for reasoning about whether the action would cause the aim to be fulfilled. An analysis of how to reason about cause and effect is given in *Cause and Effect, Conditionals, Explanation* in this series. Briefly, we can state a purported cause with a claim A that describes the world, and we can state a purported effect with a claim B. Then there is cause and effect if "A therefore B" is a good causal inference relative to obviously true claims that are invoked as normal conditions. The usual necessary and, in practice, sufficient conditions for a causal inference to be good are the following.

Necessary conditions for cause and effect For a particular causal claim to be true, describing the purported cause with a claim A and purported effect with a claim B, the following must hold:

- Both A and B are true.
- Given the normal conditions, the inference from A to B is valid or strong.
- Given the normal conditions and perhaps other plausible claims, the inference from B to A is valid or strong.
- A is true of an earlier time than B, and both are true of particular places.
- There is no common cause of both A and B.

Colloquially, conditions (1–5) are:

- A and B both happened.
- It's (nearly) impossible for A to have happened and B not to happen.
- If A hadn't happened, B wouldn't have happened (the cause makes a difference).

- A happened before B happened.
- There is no common cause.

But here we aren't investigating whether the action did cause the aim to be fulfilled. We want to know whether the action would cause the aim to be filled.

Hypothetical causal claims Suppose we have a causal claim about what could have happened in the past or might happen in the future, where the purported hypothetical cause can be described by a claim A and the purported effect by a claim B. The necessary conditions for the causal inference from A to B to be good are that for every way in which A could have been or could become true:

1. B becomes true at a later time than A.
2. The inference from A to B is valid or strong.
3. The inference from B to A is valid or strong.
4. There is no D that would describe a common cause of A and B which would be true in the hypothesized description of the world.

Condition (1) reflects that the cause and the effect cannot be simultaneous, which will be fulfilled so long as the action and the fulfillment of the aim are not simultaneous.[13] Thus, "You should do α in order to α" will be false, which is consistent with our analysis in Example 66.

Condition (4) requires that there is no common cause. In this context this means that there is no other claim that is or will be true that entails both the action being done and the aim being fulfilled. I believe this condition is covered by requiring, as we already have, that it be possible for the person not to do the prescribed action.

We've seen above that it's too much to require that a prescribed action would fulfill an aim. What we accept normally is that the prescribed action is more likely to fulfill the aim than other options. That is, the causal inference is better than ones for the other options.

Comparing actions for how likely they are to fulfill an aim
Doing X is *more likely to fulfill aim* α than doing Y if:

- A_α would not become true at the same time as A_X.
- The inference "A_X therefore A_α" relative to the normal conditions is stronger than the inference "A_Y therefore A_α."

If X is more likely to fulfill the aim than any other option under consideration, then it will yield the best causal inference among the options. Since one of those options is doing nothing, condition (3) — that the cause makes a difference—is respected, too.

As I discuss in "Arguments" and in "Probabilities" in *The Fundamentals of Argument Analysis*, the evaluation of the strength of an inference is not susceptible in general to a probability analysis; we have only an informal analysis of the evaluation of the strength of inferences. However, that kind of informal analysis is needed throughout all of our reasoning and is not peculiar to reasoning with prescriptive claims or cause and effect.

3. Evaluating options for action

Much of the evaluation of personal "should"-claims for a specified aim depends on the preferences and abilities of the person to whom the claim is addressed. But not all.

Example 67   Hubert is suffering from what the doctors say is terminal cancer of the lungs. He's smoked since he was thirteen, and though he stopped last year his doctors say that there's no chance the cancer won't kill him within one year.

> Louise: You should get some of that extract of apricot pits. You can get it in Tijuana, and there's a chance it will cure your cancer.
>
> Beth: If you go to Tijuana, you'll be wasting your money and your time. The apricot-pit cure has been discounted by all of the medical profession in the U.S. as having absolutely no effect whatever on cancer. You shouldn't try the apricot-pit cure.
>
> Hubert: Yes, yes, Beth, I know that. But I'm going to do it. What other chance do I have?

Analysis   Here the aim for Hubert is clear: get cured. He holds that aim extraordinarily highly.

Beth points out that there is no chance that doing what Louise's "should"-claim prescribes will help Hubert achieve his aim. Though Hubert acknowledges that Beth's argument is good, he won't accept her conclusion. His hopes overwhelm his reasoning. Does that mean Louise's claim is not bad advice/false?

Even in this context of personal preferences, we don't want to countenance complete incompetence in evaluating a claim. If Hubert won't reason well, that doesn't mean that Louise and Beth have to reason badly, too. We needn't expect Hubert to be a perfect reasoner, exactly calculating the degree to which a particular course of action could achieve his aims. But we do expect that he is minimally capable of reasoning well: if he accepts that an argument is good, he'll accept that the conclusion is true. Beth is right. Doing what the "should"-claim prescribes won't help Hubert achieve his aim. So the claim is bad advice/false.

Here's a summary of what we've seen about comparing options.

Comparing options for achieving a specified aim for a personal "should"-claim

Doing X is *a better option for a person to achieve* α than doing Y means that weighing the following according to the person's preferences and abilities, and reasoning well, X ranks higher than Y:

- Whether X is more likely to achieve α than Y.
- Whether X is easier to do than Y.
- Whether X is likely to achieve α at a more propitious time than Y.

---

4. Necessary conditions for the truth of a personal "should"-claim for a specified aim

Here are the conditions we've seen are necessary for the truth of a personal "should"-claim.

For a personal "should"-claim with specified aim
"You should do X in order to α" to be true:

1. a. It is possible for the person to whom the claim is addressed to do X.
   b. It is possible for the person to whom the claim is addressed not to do X.
2. Aim α is not incompatible with some other aim β that the person holds as highly.
3. Doing X is not incompatible with some other aim β that the person holds as highly.
4. X is a (part of a) better option for the person to achieve α than any other option the person is aware of.

The parenthetical remark for (4) is there because of what we saw with Example 38, which led to the definition of "part of" on p. 25.

For a personal "should"-claim with a specified aim, the options for action and the aims that need to be considered are those that the person to whom the claim is addressed is aware of. In those contexts, the aims and options that the other people in the situation have can also enter into a discussion that leads to a better evaluation of the claim. But it would be strange to say that "You should close the window" is false (Example 56) because unbeknownst to Dick, Zoe, Manuel, and Maria there is a million-dollar diamond ring on the outside window sill and if the window is closed it will fall off and be hidden under leaves and then be raked up and thrown away. Yes, Dick may value the aim "Get rich" more highly than "Get temporary relief from my backache," but it won't enter into his evaluation if he doesn't see how it is connected to the options he is considering. It would also be strange to say that "You should close the window" is false because Dick and Zoe have a heating pad they got from Dick's mother a year ago which would better alleviate Dick's back cramps, when they've both forgotten they have it. In situations like these, the person to whom the claim is addressed is trying to decide whether he or she should follow the advice/believe the claim. A person can decide what to do or not to do only on the basis of what he or she is aware of.

Before we can consider whether these conditions might be sufficient, we have to see whether they really are determinant in all cases.

5. Dilemmas

Example 68 Beth: What are you going to do about breeding the
                          sheep this year?
          Sam: I want to get a good crop of lambs. Perhaps I'll just keep
                          the ram we've got.
          Beth: You should get a new one. That one is too old.

Analysis Sam has to decide whether Beth's advice is good. He reckons that the ram they have will probably do well enough, though the ram is getting old and might not breed with all the ewes. But he's given good lambs for several years now, and it's easy to deal with him, and there wouldn't be the bother of getting a new ram. On the other hand, their neighbor Sarah knows a fellow about three hours' drive away who's got a great ram of the right breed. She's seen it, and the guy wants to sell it because he's got too many rams. That ram showed it could breed well last year and would certainly do better than Sam's old one. But it's a real bother to take a day off to get the ram, and then

Sam would have to sell his old one and get the new ram used to him. Sam just can't decide.

The two options—doing nothing amounts to keeping the old ram— seem equally good to Sam. One's easier but less likely to fulfill his aim; the other is harder but more likely to fulfill his aim. Sam doesn't have a strong preference one way or the other. So he can't decide. Does that mean the claim is neither good advice/true nor bad advice/false?

On reflection, Sam will find that he does have a preference. And if he doesn't make sufficient reflection, never getting around to thinking hard about it, just one day finding that he's left it too late and his old ram is now breeding, that doesn't mean that Beth's claim isn't true or false. It just means that Sam didn't bother to reflect enough to find out which it is.

Example 69   Last week Beth's father was hit by a drunken driver when he was crossing the street at a crosswalk. He's in the hospital, severely injured, with no hope of ever getting out of bed. The doctors say he'll always be in very bad pain. He's hooked up to machines that keep him breathing and alive, though he can still communicate with effort. He says to Beth:

> You should disconnect the machines in order to let me die
> without suffering more and in at least a little dignity before
> I deteriorate further.

Analysis   The prescribed action will fulfill the aim, and it is possible for Beth to do it or not do it. Beth, however, considers not only the specified aim, which she holds very highly, but her other aims as well. She holds equally highly the aim to treat all life as sacred and never contribute to the death of anyone. If she follows her father's advice, she will not fulfill that aim.

Beth has a *dilemma*: she holds two aims equally highly, but to fulfill one precludes fulfilling the other. She can't revert to the default of doing nothing because in this case to do nothing is to fulfill one of the aims and not the other.

It seems that in this case the conditions for the truth of a personal "should"-claim with specified aim given above are not determinant. Is there, then, no further condition that we can invoke that will let us classify Beth's father's claim as good advice/true or bad advice/false?

We still want to be able to reason with her father's claim, for example: if you should turn off the machines, then she should do it quickly; if you should follow your father's wishes, then you should turn off the machine. We reason with the sentence as a claim, as being either true or false. The difficulty is for Beth to determine which it is. But it seems that if her own preferences do not determine whether it is true or false, there is no further condition she or anyone else can invoke. We have, then, two choices for how to proceed.

(1) We can say that the claim is indeed a dilemma. Seemingly, the conditions for it to be true as well as the conditions for it to be false are both satisfied.[14]

We agree to view the sentence as a claim in order to determine whether it is true or whether it is false. But in doing so, we find that the truth-conditions for it are indeterminate. We cannot say that the sentence is both true and false without abandoning all our methods of reasoning, including those that led us to that conclusion. So we no longer take the sentence to be a claim.

This option is not peculiar to prescriptive claims. We take the descriptive sentence "This sentence is false" to be a claim, and in reasoning with it we find that if it is true then it is false, and if it is false then it is true. When we realize that, then we no longer agree to view it as a claim. We call such a purported descriptive claim a *paradox*, whereas we call such a purported prescriptive claim a dilemma.

Such sentences are then outside the scope of our theory. However, as with the liar paradox, we may be able to extend our theory to deal with them by modifying the conditions for a prescriptive claim to be true by paying attention to parts of our experience that we ignored in first establishing our theory.[15]

(2) We can say that this example, as all personal "should"-claims that are dilemmas, is only an apparent tie. Sufficient reflection by Beth will allow her to see which of these two aims she values more highly. The claim is good advice/true or bad advice/false; it just isn't immediately clear to Beth what her preferences are that determine that. There is no reason to think that we can easily and rapidly evaluate every personal "should"-claim with specified aim. This is not to say that Beth unconsciously values one aim more highly than the other. It is only to say that on sufficient reflection she will come to view one of the aims more highly than the other. And this is not an idle speculation, for if she does nothing, that will fulfill one of the aims and not the other. So she does need to make a choice.

Example 70 Ruth is desperately in love with Harold. She thinks of him day and night, and he loves her as desperately. But she is engaged to Ronald. She is talking with her close friend Barbara:

Barbara: You should marry Harold.

Ruth: Why?

Barbara: So you can be forever with the one man you love.

Ruth: But then I would have to break my engagement to Ronald, and I would never be able to respect myself, knowing how I had broken his heart, and broken my word to him, and gone against my father's wishes.

Analysis Is Barbara's claim good advice/true?

Ruth has two aims which are incompatible: to live with the man she loves and to live with her own self-respect. She holds both aims equally highly. Her options are to marry Harold, marry Ronald, or do nothing. If she does nothing, she fulfills neither aim, and that seems a worse option.

Most of us, I suspect, have a hard time imagining this is a real dilemma. We think it is obvious that one way of acting will be preferable to the other for some reason not considered in the example. Most likely, though, that's because we're imagining ourselves in Ruth's place and are using our own preferences in place of hers to evaluate the claim.

But still we imagine that Ruth will find one of the options better. Perhaps she will begin to consider marrying neither of the men to be best in order to fulfill the aim of living in the peace of knowing that she hasn't harmed either one more than the other and hasn't harmed her father. Or she will begin to value her love more highly than her honor. Or her honor more highly than her love. All we know of people is likely to convince us that she will not live with such a dilemma long. Knowing that doing nothing is an option, she considers that, too, so that we cannot say that she falls willy-nilly into a course of action.

Still, it might be a real dilemma. As Bas C. Van Fraassen says[16]:

> If two duties, equally sacred, conflict, an exercise of the will can settle the conflict, but not a calculation of values.

6. A personal element in truth
The truth or falsity of a personal "should"-claim for a specified aim depends on the preferences of the person to whom it is addressed. Yet it is not just those preferences but the process of evaluation that

determines the truth-value of the claim. As the person to whom it is addressed mulls the various aims and options, considering more, weighing and judging, the claim becomes true or false. It seems, then, that the claim on being uttered is not yet true or false. But if not, how can the person reason with it when trying to evaluate it?

We seem to be in a place that is not encountered in other ways of reasoning. A sentence isn't true or false but becomes true or becomes false by the personal intervention of someone considering his or her own preferences or possible actions that he or she could do.

Yet this is not unusual. Consider the evaluation of the strength of an inference in trying to decide if an argument is good. We have to ask whether it is likely that the premises could be true and conclusion false. We evaluate possibilities according to our own standard of what is likely, though that evaluation almost always turns out to be shared by others after sufficient discussion among those concerned in evaluating the inference. Should we say that "This inference is strong" is not true or false when uttered but becomes so only after sufficient reflection by one or more people?

The problem of whether an utterance is true or false from the moment it is spoken or only after someone, or some group of people, or some creature (Spot the dog smelling two bowls of dog food) makes an evaluation is endemic to all reasoning in which there is a personal element. But it is a problem only if we adopt an attitude that the conditions for whether a sentence is true or false are satisfied or not at the moment the sentence is uttered. That standard seems not to be fulfilled in the examples above. But the adoption of that standard is also at issue.

Claims about the future have a similar problem. We all use and treat sentences such as "It will rain tomorrow" and "Dick will marry Zoe next year" as true or false. Does this mean we commit ourselves to the view that everything in the world is determined in advance in order for those sentences to have a truth-value now?

The definition of "claim" I use is meant to avoid taking a stand on these issues. A sentence is a claim if we agree to view it as true or false. In all these cases it simplifies our reasoning enormously to view such sentences as true or false from the start of our consideration of them. If you wish, you can say that a proposition, for example, is what is true or false, and then what we are doing in our reasoning is establishing whether a particular sentence represents or correlates to a proposition. But then you are faced with explaining what a proposition is, and how, if it is not the utterance in context, it can and does play a role in our reasoning. My sense is that invoking such propositions only serves to make it possible for those who want complete impersonality in their reasoning to have an object that is true or false, even when that object has no other role than marking a place we want to get to in our reasoning. More apt is to say that we reason with sentences as if they are true or false and in doing so come to an evaluation of which they are: true or false.

7. Good reasoning and evaluating preferences

Example 71   Dick: That was a great meal. How about some dessert?

    Zoe: We've got ice cream.

    Dick: Great.

    Zoe: Which would you like: strawberry, chocolate, or vanilla?

    Dick: Boy, that's a hard decision.

    Zoe: You exasperate me. You should have vanilla.

Analysis   Zoe's claim has the unstated but obvious aim that Dick should enjoy his dessert. The problem is that Dick prefers strawberry to chocolate, and he prefers chocolate to vanilla, but he also prefers vanilla to strawberry.

Here there's no question of Dick not knowing his preferences nor being unclear about the options for action or their consequences. The problem is that his own valuation of aims is circular. Though some say that it is irrational of Dick to have circular preferences, there's nothing unusual nor wrong in doing so except that it prevents an idealized probability calculus from being applied. It is Dick's preferences that have to be taken into account in determining the truth-value of the claim. That those preferences are circular do not make him a bad reasoner, for reasoning is not involved in his holding them.

In any case, this is only a theoretical problem, not a true dilemma. Dick will decide for one of the flavors rather than going without ice cream. Perhaps some other aspect of the situation will show up to tilt his preferences—perhaps they're almost out of vanilla and he should finish off the carton. Or he'll just settle for one of the flavors. Neither Dick, nor any of us, is a good candidate to be Buridan's ass.

Example 72   Zoe: We should get a new car.

    Dick: You know we don't have enough money for a new car.

Zoe: I mean a different car, a used one in better shape than ours.
Dick: Why?
Zoe: Because it broke down again today when I was at the grocery, and I had to get a guy there to help me push start it.
Dick: Oh, that's the starter motor again. We can get Mohammed to replace it.
Zoe: Sure. And then get new tires. And a new radiator. Pretty soon it'll be costing us as much as getting a newer car.
Dick: But it's better to have ours and know what's right and wrong with it than getting another person's problems.
Zoe: Bob's AutoMart is reputable, and I figure we can get a good used car there. It'll cost a bit, but not as much as fixing up ours over a few years.
Dick: I don't know. Let's think about it.

Analysis Here the personal "should"-claim is addressed to two people, Zoe and Dick. The aim, though unstated, is clear: to have a reliable car at the minimal cost, both in money and trouble.

The problem is that to evaluate which is the best option requires considering the possible consequences of each action. That is, Zoe and Dick have to consider what claims would likely become true if they buy a new car or keep the old one. That kind of causal evaluation is difficult and often leaves people stymied or making a bad choice because they have incomplete information and aren't good at such reasoning.

That Dick and Zoe don't have all the information they need and aren't perfect reasoners doesn't mean that their evaluation of the "should"-claim will be wrong or unjustified. For a personal "should"-claim with specified aim, we expect the person to be a competent reasoner but not a perfect reasoner. Just how good a reasoner we might expect the person to be is an issue we'll consider below. Even a great reasoner, the very best, can't survey all options, all consequences, and all aims. Here it is Dick and Zoe's evaluation that will determine the truth-value of the claim, imperfect though that may be.[17]

8. Truth-conditions for a personal "should"-claim for a specified aim

We have seen necessary conditions for a personal "should"-claim with specified aim to be true. I propose that we take them to be sufficient as well.

Truth-conditions for a personal "should"-claim with specified aim
"You should do X in order to α" is true if and only if:

1. a. It is possible for the person to whom the claim is addressed to do X, and he or she knows that.
   b. It is possible for the person to whom the claim is addressed not to do X, and he or she knows that.
2. Aim α is not incompatible with some other aim β that the person is aware of and holds as highly.
3. Doing X is not incompatible with some other aim β that the person is aware of and holds as highly.
4. X is a (part of a) better option for the person to achieve α than any other option the person is aware of.

Further examples over time will either confirm these conditions as sufficient or raise more conditions that are needed for the truth of personal "should"-claims. In the meantime, let's consider them apt.

Note that all the truth-conditions for a personal "should"-claim with a specified aim are descriptive. If one of them were prescriptive, we would have to give the truth-conditions for that, which would involve another prescriptive claim, and so on forever.

Note also that in evaluating a personal "should"-claim with a specified aim we do not necessarily endorse the person's aim(s). We are considering only whether the advice is good relative to that particular person's aim(s). Thus, "You should kill that dog" might be good advice if someone's aim is to kill all dogs, even though that aim is reprehensible. We'll consider below how to factor into our analyses consideration of other people's valuations of aims.

9. Personal "should"-claims without specified aim
The examples of "should"-claims we've seen either have an aim that is explicitly specified or an aim that is obvious in the context. But often we state "should"-claims without specifying any aim.

Example 73 Beth: Look, someone's abandoned another puppy near our gate.
Sam: Another one? Why do people leave their dogs out here in the country?
Beth: You should take it to the animal shelter.

Analysis   This is a "should"-claim addressed to a particular person, Sam, with his and Beth's aims the only ones meant to be considered. But what aims?

Possibly Beth had no specific aim in mind when she made her claim. Does that mean what she said is too vague to be true or false? Consider how Beth and Sam continued to discuss her claim.

Sam: Why?
Beth: We can't keep it, and it isn't right to let him die.
Sam: But we could use another dog, and this one looks like it could be a good sheep dog. I swear it's a border collie.
Beth: We need to have fewer animals, not more.

When Sam asks "Why?" he's requesting Beth to specify an aim. But they don't stop there. They begin to survey all their relevant aims along with how various options might fulfill those. They do so because they think that the original statement is a claim.

When no aim is specified, a personal "should"-claim is meant as open to investigation of all aims. Then it's true if for one of those aims all the truth-conditions hold.

Truth-conditions for a personal "should"-claim without specified aim

"You should do X" is true if and only if:

E   There is an aim which the person(s) to whom the claim is addressed has and is aware of such that:

Conditions (1)–(4) for the truth of a personal "should"-claim with specified aim are satisfied.

The existential clause here is constructive: it is not enough that there is an aim that no one knows about or that the person to whom the claim is addressed is ignorant of. The aim must be picked out explicitly in order for the claim to be true.

Alternatively, we can resolve how to reason with personal "should"-claims without a specified aim by using a linguistic equivalence.

Personal "should"-claims without a specified aim

"You should do X" will be analyzed as (assimilated to):

"There is an aim α you have such that you should do X in order to α."

We don't need to say that the two sentences mean the same, but only that we can (agree to) use the latter in place of the former, so long as the existential clause is understood to be constructive.

The evaluation of a personal "should"-claim proceeds the same whether the aim is specified initially or not except for where we stop in the evaluation. For "You should do X in order to α," we stop and say it is false if, for example, doing X would not fulfill α, even though in the meantime we had considered other aims. For "You should do X," we continue the evaluation to see if doing X would fulfill another aim β so that "You should do X in order to β" is true.

Example 74 Zoe is baby-sitting and is getting ready to put to bed her neighbor's six-year old daughter Flo.

  Flo: You should leave a light on in the room.
  Zoe: Why?
  Flo: Because if you don't the monsters will come out from
         under the bed and hurt me.
  Zoe: But there aren't any monsters. See, I've looked under
         the bed.
  Flo: But there are, there are. I'll never sleep.
  Zoe: O.K., I'll leave a light on.

Analysis Zoe accepts "You should leave a light on" not because of the aim that Flo specifies but because of an aim Zoe holds: to help Flo sleep. The claim "You should leave the light on in the room in order to keep monsters from hurting Flo" is false because doing the action won't make a difference in achieving the aim. But "You should leave the light on in the room in order to help Flo sleep" is true, and hence "You should leave the light on in the room" is true.

10. "Should"-claims for a particular person: personal, interpersonal, and impersonal standards
Many "should"-claims, though directed to a particular person, are not meant to be evaluated relative to only that person's aims and capabilities.

Example 75 Zoe and Maria are looking on as Manuel and Dick play chess. Zoe says Maria:

  Dick should move his Queen. Then it's checkmate in two.

  Analysis Zoe is not telling Dick what he should do; the rules of the game don't allow that. Zoe is saying what the best action for Dick is, relative to what she perceives to be his aim: to win the game.

The analysis of "should"-claims we've developed is not appropriate here. Dick may be unaware that if he moves his Queen it will be checkmate in two. But that doesn't mean the claim is false. The options and the likelihood of their fulfilling Dick's aim that need to be considered in the evaluation of the claim include those that Zoe and Maria can see, not just the ones that Dick is aware of.

Example 76 (Example 47 again)

> Dick: What are you doing?
> Dogcatcher: This dog just bit a child. I'm going to take it to
>   the shelter and put it down.
> Dick: You shouldn't kill that dog.
> Manuel: Yes, you should kill it.
> Dogcatcher: Yes, I should kill it.

Analysis Manuel and Dick are telling the dogcatcher what she should do. So it seems that the analysis should be for a personal "should"-claim. But Dick, Manuel, and the dogcatcher do not think that "You should kill that dog" is true or false depending on only the dogcatcher's aims. That would be to put her particular aims above any that might hold more generally. Killing dogs would then be good or bad according to personal whim.

No, as Manuel, Dick, and the dogcatcher reason together, they will say that they have certain aims they believe are behind their "should"s. The dogcatcher says, "Always follow the rules and laws of this city." Manuel will say, "Kill any dog that is vicious." Dick will say, "Never kill a dog." Those are understood by these people not as personal aims but as aims that are meant for everyone. These folks certainly do not believe that "You should kill that dog" is true when meant for the dogcatcher and false when meant for Dick.

Every aim we considered in the previous sections was a personal aim: it is held by a particular person for a motive, and there is no reason to think that other people, even in the situation in which the claim is made, share that aim or motive.

An aim is interpersonal if most people hold it as a personal aim for roughly similar reasons. When we claim that an aim is interpersonal, we believe that it is good for everyone, and that everyone will aim for what is good for himself or herself. "Thou shalt not kill" is a good interpersonal aim, we might say, meaning it is an aim that is good for all of us, one that all of us should reckon in evaluating what we should do, and one we should all be aware of. We could try to justify this by arguing that some aims are universally good for everyone, invoking usually some other aim that seems even more clearly good as the basis of that, for example, "Live in a harmonious society."

In the last example Dick does not think his aim is personal or interpersonal. He offers it as an impersonal aim: it is good for everyone regardless of their particular beliefs or circumstances. It is good because of some standard independent of people, in this case because Dog tells us to act that way.

Personal, interpersonal, and impersonal aims

An aim is *personal* if it is held by a particular person for a reason peculiar to him or her.

An aim is *interpersonal* if most people hold it as a personal aim for roughly similar reasons.

An aim is *impersonal* if it is good for everyone regardless of their particular beliefs or circumstances.

Example 77 Mother: You shouldn't eat with your fingers here
in public.
Flo: Why not? That guy over there is doing it.
Mother: It's not what we do. Polite people don't do that.

Analysis Flo's mother's aim, which she is trying to instill in Flo, is to act in accord with the standards of polite conduct. She knows it isn't an aim that nearly all people hold. But it's a standard and aim she thinks is shared by the group of people she wants Flo to be part of: "polite society."

We can say that an aim is **group specific interpersonal** if most people in a particular group hold it as a personal aim for roughly similar reasons. In what follows I won't point out this standard when it's being used if it's clear what group is intended, treating it as a restricted kind of interpersonal standard. If we want to stress that the group is all people, we can say the aim is **universal**.

Example 78   Zeke: Jeez, I really hate dogs.

> Zoe: Even so, you shouldn't kick that puppy. It's cruel, and it's wrong to hurt animals needlessly. Think what our society would come to if we all gave way to our cruel impulses with animals. That would carry over to our relations with other people, and we would have a harsh, cruel world to live in.

> Dick: I agree, but there's a better reason why you shouldn't hurt animals needlessly, particularly dogs. Each has a soul, and it's wrong to torture anything that has a soul.

> Zeke: Well, I hate dogs and that's good enough for me.

(A fight ensues as Dick and Zoe try to restrain Zeke while the puppy looks on.)

Analysis   Here we see each kind of aim. Zeke holds a personal aim: hurt what I hate. Zoe's aim is "Don't hurt animals needlessly," which she argues is interpersonal. Dick holds the same aim but gives a reason to think it's impersonal.

For each "should"-claim we have a choice of what kind of aims we intend to be considered in its evaluation:

your aims   *personal*

our aims   *interpersonal*

the aims   *impersonal*

For each "should"-claim, we have a choice of whether we have a personal or impersonal standard for considering options:

the options *you* are aware of   *personal*

the options *we* are aware of   *interpersonal*

the options   *impersonal*

The personal "should"-claims in the examples in previous sections were meant to be judged relative to personal aims and options. The examples in this section are meant to be evaluated relative to interpersonal or impersonal aims and/or options, ones that the person to whom the "should"-claim is directed might not even be aware of. "Should"-claims used in this way to invoke impersonal norms are **normative**.[18]

It's hard to evaluate "should"-claims that are meant to be normative. First, an aim has to be established. That is, an argument must be made or insight shared that a particular aim, whether it be personal, as in Example 75, or interpersonal, or impersonal, as in Examples 76 and 78, is the correct one relative to which the claim should be judged. The existential clause is still constructive.

We also have to decide whether we intend all possible aims to be considered in trying to evaluate whether the prescribed action is incompatible with an aim that has higher value, and we also have to evaluate how important achieving the aim is. Indeed, we have to decide what "has greater value" means. Value, on the face of it, is not something that is impersonal, but some people believe it is. With normative claims it seems that we mean that values of aims are meant to be judged at least by some interpersonal standard. But the chess example shows that this need not be the case, for it is only Dick's aim there that matters.

We also have to decide in evaluating the options for fulfilling the aim whether those are meant to be judged relative to a single person's capacities and preferences or by some impersonal standard.

Difficult as such an evaluation may be, we can nonetheless state the truth-conditions for "should"-claims directed to a particular person by modifying the truth-conditions for personal "should"-claims to take into account the variety of aims and options that might be considered.

Truth-conditions for "You should do X in order to α" for a particular person

"You should do X in order to α" is true if and only if:

1. a. It is possible for you to do X
      and [you know that/we know that/ —].
   b. It is possible for you not to do X
      and [you know that/we know that/ —].

2. Aim α is not incompatible with some other aim β
   [you are aware of/we are aware of/ —] that is as valuable
   [to you/to us/ —].

3. Doing X is not incompatible with some other aim β
   [you are aware of/we are aware of/ —] that is as valuable
   [to you/to us/ —].

4. X is a (part of a) better option for you to achieve α than any
   other option Y [you know/we know/ —]. That is, weighing
   the following, X ranks higher [to you/to us/ —]:

    a. Whether X is more likely to achieve α than Y.
    b. Whether X is easier to do than Y.
    c. Whether X is likely to achieve α at a more propitious
       time than Y.

In evaluating a "should"-claim we can use any mix of personal, interpersonal, or impersonal standards. The word "you" in a part of the analysis indicates a personal standard; "we" indicates an interpersonal standard (perhaps relative to a specific group); "—" indicates no condition is imposed, that is, an impersonal standard. Which sort of standards we choose to use to evaluate the "should"-claim will be determined in part by context. It doesn't seem likely that we can state with much precision what kinds of contexts determine which kinds of standards.

But it might not be just context. What it may come down to is what a person proposes should be the way to evaluate a particular prescriptive claim or all prescriptive claims. We can't evaluate that "should" according to the analyses we've proposed, for how to evaluate that one, too, is at stake. There is no way out of the circle except to say that this is how we shall evaluate such a claim for whatever reasons we propose. Those reasons will be relative to certain aims, and we can reason about them using the conversion methods described previously. I will discuss this more in examples below.

We also have an evaluation of "should"-claims where no aim is specified.

"Should"-claims for a particular person without a specified aim
"You should do X" will be analyzed as (assimilated to) "There is an aim α [you have/we have/—] such that you should do X in order to α."

---

11. Further kinds of "should"-claims
In Section A we looked at several kinds of "should"-claims. Let's see how consideration of aims can be factored into their analyses.

a. General "should" claims
As discussed in Section A.11, we often intend the "you" in "You should do X" to be taken as meaning everyone. We considered the following.

G   "You should do X" meant to apply to all people and all times
is true if and only if "For any person in any context, that person
should do X" is true.

But it isn't clear what aim or aims are meant to be invoked.

We might consider (G) to be completely relativized. That is, the
general "should"-claim is true if and only if each claim "You should do
X" for a particular person and context is evaluated as true relative to the
particular aim(s) of that person. There is not one single aim relative to
which the claim is meant to be judged. For example, "You should
refrain from killing dogs" could be true due to there being millions of
distinct aims people have relative to which "You should refrain from
killing dogs" turns out to be true in each individual case. We treat the
general "should"-claim as summarizing all particular "should"-claims.
This is what we call a *fully relativized general "should"-claim*.

Normally, though, when we make a general claim, like "You
should refrain from killing dogs," we intend there to be just one aim
relative to which it is meant to be judged, say, "Treat dogs as sacred."
In that case, too, we will have to consider all aims of all people, but
there is some hope that a general analysis, one that depends on the
nature of people or their society or the gods, will show that for each
person clause (4) of the truth-conditions holds. In that case, we can
specify the single aim or simply hold that there is one, whether it be
interpersonal or impersonal. On these understandings, we can make the
following definitions, noting that it is only by context or by asking the
person making the claim that we can resolve which aim is meant.

General "should"-claims for a specified aim   "You should do X
in order to α" meant to apply to all people and all times is true if and
only if "You should do X in order to α" is true for each person and
each context in which the person might be.

General "should"-claims for a single unspecified aim   "You should
do X" meant to apply to all people and all times for a single unspecified
aim is true if and only if there is an aim α such that "You should do X
in order to α" is true for each person and each context in which the
person might be.

---

b. Impersonal "should" claims

Example 79   (Example 20 again)

Society should ensure that everyone has the necessities: a good place to sleep, food, clothing, and a chance to do productive work.

Analysis   In Section A.12 we said that this claim is best understood as:

> Each of us should do what we can towards ensuring that everyone in our society has the necessities: a good place to sleep, food, clothing, and a chance to do productive work.

To do so amounts to taking what appears to be a prescription to be instead an aim for each of us, with "what you can" being a kind of variable meant to be filled out by considering what each individual person can or cannot do that might or might not fulfill that aim. That is, *a prescription for a society becomes an aim for each individual.*

c. "Shouldn't"

Aims also have to be factored into the evaluation of negations. The negation of "You should do X" in the sense of "It's not the case that you should X" is true when "You should do X" is false, and false when "You should do X" is true. So if the claim is meant for a particular "you," there is no aim that will make all the truth-conditions for "You should do X" hold.

Example 80   Dick: You should go to the dance tonight.
         Manuel: Why?
         Dick: I don't know. It just seems like a good idea.
         Manuel: It doesn't seem like a good idea to me.

Analysis   Dick can't specify an aim relative to which Manuel should judge "You should go to the dance tonight," and, since Manuel doesn't have such an aim, Manuel reckons that "You should go to the dance tonight" is bad advice/false. That is, "It's not the case that you should go to the dance tonight" is true. This is one way that Dick's claim can fail to be true.

In contrast, "You should refrain from doing X" is an atomic "should"-claim, with the usual truth-conditions (pp. 65–66):

> There is an aim α [you have/we have/—] such that:
> 1. a. It is possible for you to refrain from doing X
>   and [you know that/we know that/—].

    b. It is possible for you not to refrain from doing X
       and [you know that/we know that/ —].

2. Aim α is not incompatible with some other aim β
   [you are aware of/we are aware of/ —] that is as valuable
   [to you/to us/ —].

3. Refraining from doing X is not incompatible with some
   other aim β [you are aware of/we are aware of/ —] that is
   as valuable [to you/to us/ —].

4. Refraining from doing X is a (part of a) better option for you to
   achieve α than any other option Y [you know/we know/ —].
   That is, weighing the following, X ranks higher [to you/to us/ —]:

    a. Whether refraining from doing X is more likely to
      achieve α than Y.

    b. Whether refraining from doing X is easier to do than Y.

    c. Whether refraining from doing X is likely to achieve α
      at a more propitious time than Y.

Compare these conditions with the truth-conditions for "You should do X." The aim relative to which the claim is meant to be judged may be different from the one for "You should do X." In Example 57 we evaluate "You should close the window" relative to Dick's aim of getting warmer. We evaluate "You should refrain from closing the window" relative to Maria's aim of not making the room hot and stuffy. However, in the evaluation of both "You should do X" and "You should refrain from doing X" we normally consider a range of aims in the analysis so that in the end we have to look at the same aims and causal inferences. In particular, in evaluating "You should do X" we consider the option of not doing X, that is, refraining from doing X. In evaluating "You should refrain from doing X" we consider not refraining from doing X, that is, doing X.

d. Complex prescriptive claims

Example 81 (continuing Example 57)
    Zoe: Dick, you should close the window, and Maria, you should
        turn on the fan.

Analysis One conjunct here is evaluated relative to Dick's aims, and the other relative to Maria's aims. For the classical evaluation of "and" this is true if and only if both conjuncts are true.

Example 82   (continuing Example 57)
Dick wants to get warmer and also wants to make Maria comfortable.
Zoe might say either of the following to him:

(A) You should close the window and you should turn on the fan.

(B) You should close the window and turn on the fan.

Are these equivalent?

   Analysis In evaluating either conjunct of (A), and in evaluating
(B), we consider both of Dick's aims (α) "To get warmer" and (β) "To
make Maria comfortable." Let's assume that Dick holds (α) considerably higher than (β). We consider all of the following options:

   Do nothing.
   Close the window.
   Don't close the window.
   Turn on the fan.
   Don't turn on the fan.
   Close the window and turn on the fan.

   Claim (A) is true if and only if each conjunct is true. In that case,
we could have (A) false but (B) true. The first conjunct of (A) could be
true but the second conjunct false, for the second is meant to be judged
only against the single aim (β). Yet (B) could be true in the same
circumstances because it is meant to be judged relative to the joint aim
(α and β), "To get warmer and to make Maria comfortable." So Dick
holding (α) much higher than (β) doesn't matter. Hence, "You should
do X and you should do Y" need not be equivalent to "You should do
X and do Y."

Example 83   (continuing Example 57)
   Zoe (to Dick): If you close the window, you should turn on the fan.

   Analysis Suppose "You close the window" is true. That is, Dick
closes the window. Then Maria will be hot. Then Dick must consider
the aim, "Don't make the room too hot and stuffy for Maria," which,
if he adopts it, would make "You should turn on the fan" true. But it is
certainly possible for the antecedent to be true and consequent false: it
might be too difficult to find the fan, or Dick might choose not to adopt
that aim. So it seems the conditional is false.

   But that analysis is not for the conditional. It shows that the
inference "You close the window, therefore, you should turn on the
fan" is not valid or even strong. If we are considering whether the

conditional is true according to the classical interpretation of "if . . . then . . . ", we have to ask whether the antecedent is true and consequent false, not whether it is possible for the antecedent to be true and consequent false. The only way we can verify whether that is the case here is when Dick closes the window, ask him if he's adopted that aim about Maria and determine how hard it is for him to turn on the fan. That's because Dick closing the window is not sufficient for him to adopt the aim of not making the room too hot and stuffy.

Example 84 (continuing Example 78)
   If you hate dogs, then you should kill this dog.
   Analysis We know that Zeke hates dogs, and he believes that this is sufficient for him to have the aim of killing any dog he can. But the conditional is still false. The dog belongs to the mayor, and killing it would be incompatible with Zeke's aim of not getting thrown in jail.

Example 85 (continuing Example 47)
If you should kill all vicious dogs, then you should kill this vicious dog.
   Analysis Whatever aim that will serve to make the antecedent true will also serve to make the consequent true.

Example 86 (continuing Example 47)
If you should kill this vicious dog, then you should kill all vicious dogs.
   Analysis This is false. The dogcatcher has the aim of killing all vicious dogs that are in her jurisdiction, but she doesn't hate dogs and won't try to kill vicious dogs that aren't in her city and county because she thinks that many of them can be trained to be loving and faithful. The premise is true, and the conclusion is false.

e. Second-order prescriptions

Example 87 (continuing Example 26)
   Zoe: You should follow your doctor's advice.
   Dick: Why?
   Zoe: In order to be healthy.
   Analysis We asked before whether Zoe's original claim is equivalent to the following:
      You should give up smoking cigars, and you should get more exercise, and you should get eight hours of sleep every night, and you should drink only in moderation.

If we understand prescriptions in terms of aims, the equivalence holds if and only if the aim for each of the conjuncts is "To be healthy."

Example 88   You should do what the laws say you should do.

Analysis   The law says "You should stop your car at a red light," and the aim for that is to avoid accidents; the law says "You should not wiretap without a warrant," and the aim for that is to protect privacy; the laws says . . . . We view the claim as a summing up of a range of prescriptions that we cannot (easily) specify:

> For all x (if x is a law, then you should do what x says in order to α_x).

Here α_x is an aim that the particular law x is intended to accomplish.

Perhaps, though, there is a more general aim we can invoke relative to which all laws are meant to be judged, for example, to live in a harmonious society, or to protect individual rights maximally, or . . . . Call such an aim β . In that case, we might read the claim as:

> For all x (if x is a law, you should do what x says in order to β).

But that seems wrong. We accept "You should stop your car at a red light" because of a simpler aim, and it would be very difficult to justify that claim on the basis of the more general aim. Invoking a general aim seems to require a very different reading:

> You should in order to β: for all x (if x is law, do what x says).

That is, what you should do is a quantified imperative.

12. Rationality
Debates about kinds of standards and their formulation in terms of human capacities or impersonal criteria are not normally couched in terms of how to reason about prescriptive claims. Those debates usually occur within discussions of rationality.

Example 89   (Continuing Examples 47 and 76)
>   Dick: You shouldn't kill that dog.
>   Manuel: But it would be irrational not to kill that dog.
>   *Analysis*   Manuel might just as well have said "You should kill that dog."

When "rational" or "irrational" are used in evaluating a proposed course of action, they are rarely if ever meant as tools or standards of reasoning. They are used as a value-judgment way of stating a "should"-claim. "It would be irrational not to kill that dog" sounds a lot stronger than "You should kill that dog," as if invoking some impersonal standard of reasoning that only crazy people don't adhere to. But, as I discuss in "Rationality" in this volume, there is no such standard that is being invoked. There isn't a spit of difference between "You should do X" and "Doing X is the rational thing to do," nor between "You shouldn't do X" in the sense of refraining and "It would be irrational to do X."[19]

Many analyses of the nature of rationality can be understood as attempts to give truth-conditions for (usually atomic) prescriptive claims. The value in those analyses is the close examination people make of aims and ways of fulfilling them.

Some economists use an absolute notion of rationality that surpasses human abilities, requiring a rational person to be one who considers all aims and all ways of achieving them and all the consequences of acting according to those options with no circular preferences. Others hold a similar view but considering "satisficing," that is achieving the aim, or more or less achieving the aim, rather than maximizing, which would be achieving the aim in the best possible way.[20]

Why then bother with all this talk of the truth-conditions for "should"-claims? Why not just refer to the literature on rationality as the term is used in that sense?

The analysis of prescriptive claims in terms of aims provides a framework for all those views. Each is a way to flesh out the general framework of the truth-conditions for a "should"-claim, stipulating that personal, interpersonal, or impersonal standards will be the only ones considered. The general framework allows us to make comparisons across the various viewpoints and assimilate discussions in ethics and meta-ethics to such an analysis.[21]

We'll return to questions about rationality in Section B.20.

13. Value judgments
We saw in Section A.14 that value judgments are sometimes used to make prescriptions. Words such as "good," "bad," "right," "wrong," and many others serve as markers for weighting aims. They are some help, but they are imperfect markers because it seems we can have incompatible aims that are both valued as "good" or even "best." Incompatible aims both of which we consider to be good create dilemmas, as we've seen.

Some people who discuss ethics say that "good" just means or is equivalent to "will fulfill your desires."[22] If we take "good" to be a marker we use in weighting the value of aims, this reading doesn't seem helpful. We'd have that "aim α is good" is equivalent to "achieving aim α will fulfill your desires." If we take our desires to be β, this means that "aim α is good" is equivalent to "achieving aim α will fulfill desires β," and now we have to ask whether β is good. It also isn't clear whether every desire qualifies as an aim; we would not say in English that every aim is a desire.

14. Adopting aims

In this approach to reasoning with prescriptive claims, aims are what justify our prescriptions. They are the reasons we offer for why someone should do what's prescribed. "You should do X in order to . . . ."

Often enough it will seem clear that a particular aim is appropriate. For example, one of Dick's aims is to get warmer (Example 56), and he values that a lot more highly than getting the mail from the mail box at the end of the block, though that, too, is one of his aims. It is not a problem for him to justify his aim of getting warmer. But even if he can't justify it, Zoe and Maria and Manuel are no less convinced that it is an appropriate aim for him to have. They can imagine being in his situation and they, too, would have that aim. In such cases there is no significant difference in evaluating a claim that you should do something and a claim that you should have the aim of doing that.

Example 90 (Continuing Example 56) Compare:
    a. You should close the window.
    b. You should have the aim of closing the window.

Analysis Neither of these has a specified aim. However, in context it seems that for both the implicit aim is "Get warmer." So consider the truth-conditions for these (pp. 65–66). If condition (1) holds for both, then conditions (2), (3) and (4) hold for (a) if and only if they hold for (b). So the only question is whether it is possible to do what is prescribed in these claims.

For (a) it must be possible to close the window and possible not to close the window.

For (b) it must be possible to adopt the aim of closing the window and possible not to adopt the aim of closing the window. As far as I can see, there's nothing to prevent anyone from adopting any aim.

Perhaps there are evolutionary arguments about the psychology of humans that could show that some aims cannot be adopted by people. But that certainly isn't the case here.

So if (a) is true, (b) is, too. But could (b) be true and (a) false? Suppose the window can't be closed. The truth-conditions for (b) then will not hold, too, for adopting the aim of closing the window will not in any way further the fulfillment of Dick getting warmer. It seems that the two claims are equivalent.

The example suggests the following.

The equivalence of aims and prescriptions
"You should do X in order to α" is equivalent to
"You should have the aim of doing X in order to α".

We can reason about aims by considering the corresponding prescription. Or we can reason about aims by converting them to descriptive claims, testing them for their consequences or seeing how they fulfill a more general principle. But when we do that, we're just pushing back to what we consider more fundamental aims: be consistent in your actions; judge aims by their consequences; judge aims by . . . . We may find more and more general aims that we have or shall adopt, asking always, "Why should I adopt that aim?" At some point, though, our hope of justifying our aims by reason must stop, and we are left where reason cannot go. At some point there is no further "in order to."

Example 91 (Continuing Example 78)
    Dick: You should treat dogs as sacred.
    Zeke: Why?
    Analysis Dick has no further aim relative to which his "should"-claim is meant to be judged. He says that to treat dogs as sacred is a good aim not in order to fulfill some other aim but because it is fundamental. It is an article of faith of the Church of Dog.
    In that case, the method of analysis we've adopted classifies his claim as false. For a "should"-claim to be true, it must be judged relative to some aim, and that aim cannot be the same as the action being prescribed because the justification would be circular and the prescribed action and the fulfillment of the aim would be simultaneous, as we saw in Example 66.

Example 92   (Example 19 and Example 79 again)
Society should ensure that everyone has the necessities: a good place to
sleep, food, clothing, and a chance to do productive work.

   Analysis   This claim seems so fundamental that it is hard for us to
imagine a further aim relative to which it could be judged. But if that is
the case, then by the method of analysis we've adopted, the claim is
classified as false.

   Our analysis so far is applicable only for prescriptions that can be
justified in terms of some aim. When we consider a prescription that is
equivalent to an aim that we neither can nor intend to justify in terms of
a further aim, that analysis is not applicable.

Ultimate aims   "To do X" is an *ultimate aim* [for you/for us/—]
if [you do not require or cannot give/we do not require or cannot give/
there is not required or cannot be given] a further aim that justifies
adopting it.

Ultimate prescriptive claims   "You should do X" is an *ultimate
prescriptive claim* [for you/for us/—] if and only if [you have/we
have/there is] the ultimate aim "To do X."

   Some aims that we adopt must be adopted for reasons about which
we cannot reason, though that does not mean for reasons about which
we cannot agree. When we pose that someone should adopt such an
aim, the analysis we have given for prescriptive claims in terms of aims
will fail.

   Aims are neither true nor false; they are good or bad, right or
wrong. But we have the following correspondence.

Ultimate aims related to ultimate claims   An ultimate aim being
right/wrong is equivalent to the corresponding ultimate prescription
being true/false.

   The truth or falsity of an ultimate prescriptive claim cannot be
established by an analysis of its truth-conditions in the manner for
other prescriptive claims. Its truth or falsity is given by authority,
or by revelation, or by internal searching, or by reflection, or by
society, or by a human biological imperative, or by whatever means
we countenance for determining whether an ultimate aim is good/bad

or right/wrong. Reason can take us only so far in determining what we should do. What are the good aims, the ultimate aims that we should adopt, is something our analyses here cannot touch.

15. Adopting aims: personal, interpersonal, and impersonal standards

The truth-value of an ultimate prescriptive claim depends solely on our accepting or not accepting the corresponding aim. If you/we accept the aim, or, for the impersonal case, the aim is acceptable, then the claim is true. If, for whatever reason, you/we reject the aim, or the aim is not acceptable, then the claim is false. The acceptance or rejection of the aim is beyond the scope of the methods of reasoning for prescriptive claims. Dick may reply to the query of why he believes "You should treat dogs as sacred" that he knows it from revelation. None of us can then gainsay him: as a personal "should"-claim, "You [Dick] should treat dogs as sacred" is true. That does not mean that "You [Zoe] should treat dogs as sacred" is true, or that "You [everyone] should treat dogs as sacred" is true, though those might be if we all shared his revelation. Nor does it mean that "You [Dick] should treat dogs as sacred" is true if understood as meant to be evaluated by interpersonal or impersonal standards. The truth or falsity of an ultimate prescriptive claim need not be an entirely personal matter. We have left room for the possibility of impersonal ultimate prescriptive claims.

Impersonal standards in the adoption of aims is what, apparently, Kant intended.[23] He considered two kinds of aims. There are those we have that are dependent on the situation in which we consider them. For instance,

> In the situation where Dick is cold and has back cramps and clearly wants to be without back cramps, (one of) his aim(s) is: get warm.

> In the situation where Zoe has never seen baby birds, and she wants to see baby birds, and there are baby birds in the tree next door, (one of) Zoe's aim(s) is: see a baby bird in the tree next door.

Such aims are *hypothetical imperatives*.

In contrast, a *categorical imperative* is an aim that is said not to depend on any particular situation or desire. For example:

Always tell the truth.
Don't kill dogs.
Cause no gratuitous pain.
Don't lick your plate at the dinner table.

People working in Kant's tradition would likely say that these are not categorical imperatives because they say a categorical imperative is one that is not simply good for all people and all times but is justifiably good for all people and all times, such justification being according to the standards and metaphysics they propose. For them, if "Do X" is a categorical imperative, then "You should do X" is true, not just for you or for us, but according to an impersonal standard.

Naturalists, as we discussed earlier, say that value judgments using the words "good" or "bad" are descriptive or can be reduced in some way to descriptive claims. In the analysis here, the reduction of prescriptive claims is to descriptive truth-conditions plus aims. Aims are not true or false but good or bad, and the reasons we have for adopting the fundamental ones are beyond the scope of reasoning. The analysis here is naturalism only if the conditions for an aim to be good can be given entirely in descriptive terms. Even then it seems that naturalism would require identifying the good with what you should do/should be done.

16. Necessary conditions for the truth of an ultimate prescriptive claim

We cannot specify the truth-conditions for an ultimate prescriptive claim "You should do X" in terms of other claims. But what we took as first necessary and later sufficient conditions for the truth of "You should do X in order to α" (p. 59) are necessary for ultimate prescriptive claims, too, for the same reasons as before (Section C.4). We can, however, simplify that list. The condition that doing X is not incompatible with some other aim held as highly as "Do X" is covered by requiring that "Do X" is not incompatible with some other aim that is held as highly. The condition that doing X is a better option for achieving "Do X" is trivially satisfied. Hence, we have the following.

Necessary conditions for the truth of an ultimate prescriptive claim "You should do X"
- It's possible to do X.

- It's possible not to do X.
- There is no other aim incompatible with "Do X" [you are aware of/we are aware of/ —] that is as valuable [to you/to us/ —].

Example 93 Suzy overheard Dick talking about dogs, and she says:

> You should treat all dogs as sacred or not treat all dogs as sacred.

Analysis Whether Suzy takes this as an ultimate prescriptive claim or not, it's false. It's not possible not to do what's prescribed.

Example 94 Dick patiently explains to Suzy that what she's said is false. So she says: "You should see the world exactly as a dog does."

Analysis This, too, is false, whether as an ultimate prescriptive claim or not. It's not possible to do what's prescribed, at least according to our current theories of biology, evolution, and perception.

Example 95 (Example 69 again)
Beth's father says:

> You should disconnect the machines in order to let me die
> without suffering more and in at least a little dignity before
> I deteriorate further.

Beth has two aims:

α. To let her father die without suffering more and in at least a little dignity before he deteriorates further.

β. To treat all life as sacred and never contribute to the death of anyone.

Analysis Beth's aims are incompatible, and the corresponding prescriptions are inconsistent:

A. You should let your father die without suffering more and in at least a little dignity before he deteriorates further.

B. You should treat all life as sacred and never contribute to the death of anyone.

Hence, not both of these claims can be true.

Beth holds aims (α) and (β) equally highly, even though they are incompatible. There's no reason why someone cannot hold two incompatible aims equally highly. In that case if (B) is true, then it cannot be a personal "should"-claim meant to be evaluated by personal standards, whether (B) is ultimate or not, for not holding an incompatible aim that is held as highly is necessary for its truth.

17. Possibilities

Example 96   One way the world could be is for all the following
to be true:

> Ralph is a dog.
> Ralph barks.
> Zeke hates dogs.
> Zeke should not kill Ralph.
> You should kill all vicious dogs you can.

Analysis   These claims are consistent, understanding "Zeke
should not kill Ralph" as "Not: Zeke should kill Ralph." Reading "You
should kill all vicious dogs you can" as a quantification over many
prescriptions ("You should kill this dog, and that dog, and . . ." as
in Example 27), we have that a consequence of "Ralph is a dog" and
"Ralph is vicious" and "You should kill all vicious dogs you can" is
"Zeke should kill Ralph," assuming Zeke can do that. So for this
description really to be a way the world could be, that is, to be consistent, either "Ralph is not vicious" or "Zeke is not able to kill Ralph"
must be true.

For any atomic prescriptive claim "You should do X" that is not
ultimate, a way in which it is true is one in which its truth-conditions
hold, all of which are descriptive. One of those conditions is:

> It is possible to do X.

That is, one of the conditions is itself a descriptive possibility. In this
context, this condition amounts to:

> Given a description of the world, there is a description of the
> world in the future which is consistent with that one in which
> one of the claims is "You do X."

For ultimate prescriptive claims, such as "You should treat dogs as
sacred," we have only necessary but not sufficient descriptive conditions for its truth. Assuming those are fulfilled, then, just as with the
descriptive claim "This is a rock," in our analyses of reasoning we can
go no farther than to say that the claim is true or that the claim is false.
But once we accept that an ultimate prescriptive claim is true or that it
is false, there's no more we need say when we postulate that a way the
world could be is that the claim is true.

Since truth conditions for "You should do X" when "Do X" is an ultimate aim are not analyzable, how can we say what the consequences of it are?

Compare: (‡) "This is a rock." The truth-conditions for it are not analyzable. How, then, do we know what the consequences of it are?

The consequences of (‡) are those that follow in our logic, and that is why we need to be clear about our methods of reasoning. They are also consequences of our theories. "What is a rock is not alive" is part of our implicit theory of the world, so a consequence of (‡) relative to that further assumption is "This is not alive." With ultimate prescriptive claims we can use all our usual methods of reasoning, as we discussed in Section A.

18. The Basic Rule of Consequences for prescriptive claims
Recall that in Section B.2 we investigated prescriptive inferences, that is, inferences from premises that include a prescriptive claim to a conclusion that is prescriptive. We justified and adopted the Basic Rule of Consequences for the standards approach for reasoning with prescriptive claims. We said that that is a sufficient if not necessary condition for a prescriptive inference to be valid or strong. But when we take aims into account, we need more precision in stating the rule. "You should do X" is ambiguous as to whether we mean to invoke personal, interpersonal, or impersonal standards in evaluating the claim. Let's say that a prescriptive claim meant to be analyzed by the aims approach is *personal/interpersonal/impersonal* if all of the clauses in its truth-conditions are meant to be taken as personal/interpersonal/impersonal. So taking the kinds of aims and methods of evaluation into account, we have the following.

The Basic Rule of Consequences for "should"-claims for the same specified aim
Suppose that "You should do X in order to α" and "You should do Y in order to α" are two claims both of which are personal/interpersonal/impersonal. Suppose also that doing Y is (likely) a part of doing X and you realize that/and we realize that/—. Then the following inference is valid (strong):

You should do X in order to α.
Therefore, you should do Y in order to α.

What if doing Y is part of doing X, but "You should do Y" is meant to be evaluated relative to a different aim than "You should do X"?

Example 97   (Continuing Example 57)
Dick, Zoe, Maria, Suzy, and Manuel are in Dick and Zoe's kitchen. It's cold outside, and there's a light breeze blowing in the window. They're having a good conversation and don't want to break it up, and there's no place else in their home to continue. Dick's back hurts because he's cold. So "You (Dick) should close the window" is true relative to Dick's aim "To make his back stop hurting right now." Dick also has the aim "To cure his back," which he holds very highly. Is the following a valid (strong) inference?

 (a) Dick should close the window in order to make his back stop hurting right now.
Therefore,
 (b) Dick should close the window in order to cure his back.

Analysis   The inference is weak. We've seen that (a) is true, but (b) is false: given Dick's penchant for procrastination, a better option to achieve the aim of curing his back is for him to call a physical therapist now and make an appointment. Then he can close the window. A "should"-claim need not be a consequence even of itself if evaluated relative to different aims, for there may be a better option to achieve the other aim.

Example 98   (Continuing Example 97)
Dick should close the window in order for his back to be warmer.
Therefore, Dick should get up out of his chair in order to make the blood circulate more to his back muscles.

Analysis   We know that given the circumstances, Dick getting out of his chair is a part of Dick closing the window. Moreover, any way he fulfills the aim of making his back warmer is going to be a way that he fulfills the aim of making his blood circulate more to his back muscles, as he and most of us know. Therefore, if he has the first aim, he has the second aim, too. So the inference is valid.

Example 99   (Continuing Example 97)
Dick should get up out of his chair in order to make the blood circulate more to his back muscles.
Therefore, Dick should close the window in order for his back to be warmer.

Analysis Dick closing the window isn't part of Dick getting up out of his chair. Even though Dick adopts the aim of making the blood circulate more to his back in order to fulfill the further aim of making his back warmer, the first could be true even if closing the window is a bad way to achieve that since it would make Maria unhappy. The inference is weak.

For prescriptions relative to different aims, we have the following.

The Basic Rule of Consequences for "should"-claims for different specified aims

Let "You should do X in order to α" and "You should do Y in order to β" be two claims both of which are personal/interpersonal/impersonal. Suppose that doing Y is (likely) a part of doing X and (you realize that/ and we realize that/—). Suppose also that A_β is a consequence of A_α, and that doing Y is a better option for you to achieve β than any other option (you know/we know/—). Then the following inference is valid (strong):

You should do X in order to α.
Therefore, you should do Y in order to β.

---

19. "Ought" from "is"

In the analysis of prescriptive claims in terms of standards, the following principle appeared to be correct.

H+ There is no good argument all of whose premises are descriptive and whose conclusion is prescriptive, where the prescriptive part of the conclusion appears essentially.

But this is not correct for prescriptive claims analyzed in terms of aims. Given any "should"-claim that is not ultimate, all its truth-conditions are descriptive. So the following kind of argument is good whenever the premises are plausible, as they are in many of the examples above since each premise is more plausible than the conclusion.

[All the truth-conditions for "You should do X"]
Therefore, you should do X.

Nor can we amend (H+) to rule out just the case when all the truth-conditions are present in the premises, for we could have other descriptive premises that imply those truth-conditions.

Still, (H+) holds for ultimate prescriptive claims. But that's just because no argument for such a claim is good.

20. Prescriptive claims for animals and impersonal prescriptions
Can the analysis of simple "should"-claims in terms of aims apply to animals, too?

Example 100   Beth: Look, I've trained the duckling to follow me.
  She knows she should follow me if she wants to get
  something to eat.
  Sam: Trained? She imprinted on you when her mother abandoned
  her. She'll follow you no matter what you do.

Analysis   Is "The duckling should follow Beth in order to get something to eat" true? We may feel confident we can ascribe that aim to the duckling. But as Sam points out, the duckling has no choice: it's not possible, given the circumstances, for her not to follow Beth. So the claim is false.

Our analysis of prescriptive claims in terms of aims assumes (some degree of) freedom of will, for without the ability to choose to do or not to do, all personal "should"-claims will be evaluated as false (Example 4). If animals, as Descartes claimed, are only automatons, then all atomic "should"-claims about animals meant to be evaluated with respect to their aims and capabilities are false.

Example 101   Dick and Zoe are getting ready to feed their dog Spot. They have a routine where Spot has to sit down next to his dish before he gets fed. Spot is excited and prancing around. Dick says to Zoe:

  Spot should sit down next to his dish if he wants to get fed.

Analysis   The one and only way that Spot can get fed is for him to sit down next to his dish. Dick, because of his knowledge of Spot's current and previous behavior, believes that Spot has no other aim that he holds as highly at this time which conflicts with "Get food." So, it seems to Dick, the claim is true.

For the analysis of personal "should"-claims in terms of aims to apply to animals we have to agree that we can ascribe aims to animals and, if we want to be able to evaluate the claims, we can determine which aim or aims the animal holds most highly. Those assumptions are not readily accepted by everyone. But a similar problem occurs with "should"-claims for people.

Example 102 Dick and Zoe's friend Manuel is confined to a wheel-chair with both legs nearly completely paralyzed. Dick says to Zoe: Manuel should get physical therapy for his legs.

Analysis Dick is assuming that he can ascribe aims to Manuel and that he can determine a rough but useful enough scale of value for them, either the value(s) Manuel holds or, if Dick means the claim to be inter-personal or impersonal, in terms of values we hold or impersonal values.

Example 103 Dick and Zoe have a friend Wanda who is obese.

Dick: Wanda should go on a diet. That's the only way she'll lose weight.

Zoe: No. Wanda should get psychological counseling. She has an unconscious wish to punish herself by being fat. You can see that if you talk to her.

Dick: If that's so, then there's no point in suggesting anything to Wanda because she has no choice but to follow her unconscious wishes.

Analysis Dick assumes Wanda's aim is "Lose weight," relative to which his claim is meant to be judged. But Zoe says that Wanda has an aim she holds higher, "Punish myself by eating too much." Zoe says that Wanda isn't aware of that aim, but we can see it from her behavior. Relative to an aim Zoe thinks Wanda holds more highly, "Be happy and healthy," Zoe makes her claim that Wanda should get psychological counseling. Dick argues that if Zoe is right about Wanda's unconscious wishes, then her claim is false because Wanda has no choice in the matter.

The difference between ascribing and evaluating the value of aims of animals and of people is a matter of degree—assuming you believe that animals have aims at all. We infer aims and their values by observing the behavior of people, arguing by analogy to our own internal life. We do the same for animals, only the analogy will be considerably weaker as we have less reason to believe that animals have an internal life like ours.

In some contexts people say we should evaluate a prescriptive claim relative to fully impersonal standards: the person or people to whom the claim is meant to apply need not be aware of the aims that are invoked, nor need his, her, or its capabilities be considered in evaluating the claim. That kind of analysis is sometimes invoked for prescriptive claims about animals, too.

Example 104   Tom and Manuel are out in the desert doing research for their animal ecology class. They are quietly observing three coyotes chasing a rabbit on a hill covered with shrub.

> Tom: That one coyote should take off at that angle, there, in order to cut off the rabbit, with the other two chasing the rabbit towards that spot.
>
> Manuel: And the rabbit should run into that mesquite bush to avoid the coyotes.

Analysis   Tom and Manuel have studied and know the theory of how coyotes and rabbits succeed in the wild: how they hunt, how they avoïd predators, how they get food by any means until they can breed and take care of their offspring. Their "should"-claims reflect the theories of evolutionary fitness they've studied. Such theories do not assume any reflective ability of animals, though they do take into account the capabilities of the animals being studied. The theories are meant only to predict behavior (unless Tom and Manuel have forgotten all their studies and are simply projecting onto these animals their imagination of what they themselves would do).

With this last example the "should" is not prescriptive or normative in any sense. It is the "should" of "it's most likely that." What is most likely is relative to what is predicted by the theory. A similar confusion of what is prescriptive or normative with what is descriptive occurs with claims about people.

Example 105   An economist for the Chinese government says:

> Chinese should spend less on non-durable goods and save more in this economic climate. That's the rational thing for them to do.

Analysis   Here it seems that the "should" really is normative: this is what Chinese people should do because that's what's rational. But this example is no different from the previous one. The "should" here is "it's most likely that" relative to the economic theory that defines "rational" which the economist has in mind.

We started with the idea that a prescription is a kind of advice. We began with those kinds of claims that are clearly meant to offer advice and then considered contexts where it might seem appropriate to invoke aims, or options for acting, or valuations of those options that are beyond the awareness of the people to whom the claim is addressed. For those kinds of claims, part of the "should" is that the person should be aware of those aims and options and how to properly value them. We then noted that some people consider the correct evaluation of prescriptive claims, at least in some circumstances, to be relative to impersonal standards. In those cases it is no longer even part of the prescription that the person should be aware of certain aims and options and how to evaluate them properly. That notion of "should," most common in economics and more recently in studies of animal behavior, is far from our original notion of prescriptions. That "should" is no longer one of advice but is solely "it's most likely that" relative to the given theory. It goes beyond the impersonal evaluation of normative claims to ignore even volition.

Example 106 The people around Socorro, New Mexico should stop cockfighting because it's inhumane to treat birds that way.

Analysis Part of this prescription is that those people should adopt the aims and options and valuations that are invoked by us. If you like, that means the "should" is relative to a theory, our theory of what is right and wrong.

There are two kinds of "should" and two profoundly different notions of rationality that correspond to them. The notion of "should" that is invoked by some economists and animal behaviorists, their notion of rationality, is not at all the "should" of prescriptions, the rationality of what is correct in thinking and doing. It is unfortunate that the same word "rationality" (or "should") is used for both; studying them together is as fruitful as collecting papers on law and physics in one volume because they both use the notion of force.

There is, however, an assumption that might assimilate the economists' and animal behaviorists' notion of rationality to one for prescriptive claims.

Everyone (everything) should do what is in its own best interests.

This appears to be an ultimate prescriptive claim. But it's far too vague. We need to know what is meant by "its own best interests." Economists often give such a definition in terms of their theories; when they do so, they are not doing economics but ethics. Then they have to defend that what their theory says is best for a society is also best for individuals within that society in order for our work to be applicable. Animal behaviorists also define what is in the best interest of an animal in terms of the collective, the species, relative to their theories of evolutionary fitness. Then they, too, would have to show that what is in the best interest of the species is also in the best interest of the individual for our work to be applicable. The analysis I have presented here reduces talk of collections of individuals to quantification over specific individuals. It may be possible and useful to devise an analysis of "should"-claims that are meant to be understood as applying to the collective and not to any one individual (compare Example 20).

D. Comparing Aims and Standards

When we justify a prescriptive claim by way of a base or more fundamental prescriptive claim, we infer from the general to the particular. When we analyze a prescriptive claim in terms of aims, we infer from the particular prescribed action to the general aim. What is the relation of these two analyses?

1.   Does true by virtue of aims imply true by virtue of standards?

Example 107   (Example 56 again)

>   Dick: I'm cold, cold enough that my back is starting to cramp up.
>   Zoe: You should close the window.

Analysis   We said that Zoe's claim is true on the aims analysis. The following is valid or strong given the circumstances:

>   You close the window.
>   Therefore, you get warm.

The other conditions about closing the window being the best option also hold.

How might we justify Zoe's prescription via standards? Zoe might say and Dick would agree that "You should be warmer" or, more generally, "You should not be in pain" is the standard from which "You should close the window" follows, given other appropriate claims about Dick's back cramp and pain and being warmer. Then we need that the following is valid or strong:

>   You should get warmer.
>   Therefore, you should close the window.

This will follow by the Basic Rule of consequences for prescriptive claims if the following is valid or strong:

(*)   You get warmer.
>   Therefore, you closed the window.

But (*) is weak, for there are many ways for Dick to get warmer.

Still, if we consider all the other claims we use to show that "You should close the window" is true on the aims approach, then it seems that (*) is strong, too. If there's no better option for Dick to get warmer, including doing nothing, and noting Dick abilities and attitudes, it seems that (*) is strong. But it isn't. Zoe could have closed the window. Or Maria could have lent Dick her coat. Or Manuel could have gotten Dick a hot water bottle.

The problem is that on the standards approach we have only the Basic Rule and two necessary conditions for establishing that a prescriptive claim is true. Though useful, they are not adequate. All we can say is that using the Basic Rule for the standards approach inverts the direction of inference of the aims analysis. An analysis showing that a prescriptive claim is true on the aims approach does not guarantee that the claim is true on the standards approach. We do not know sufficient conditions for a standards analysis to classify a prescriptive claim as true. Hence, given an aims analysis that shows the claim is true, we cannot conclude it would be evaluated as true on the standards approach, too.

Our general framework for reasoning with prescriptive claims on the standards approach must be fleshed out to say why we (should) accept some base prescriptive claims as true. The metaphysics then might clarify the relation between the aims and standards approach. In particular, suppose "You should do X" is true on the aims analysis relative to the aim "Do Y." We can convert that aim into "You should do Y," from which, given further claims describing the context plus some further analysis, we might be able to deduce "You should do X."

aims	*standards*
You should do X.	You should do Y.
Relative to aim "Do Y".	Therefore, you should do X.

But why should "Do Y" being acceptable/good imply that "You should do Y" is true on the standards approach? It seems we would need something like:

You should do what you want You should (on the standards approach) do whatever will best help you achieve what (you want/we want/is impersonally right to be wanted).

However, we need this only for ultimate aims since we can and if pressed must eventually reach those in our justifications. Thus, what we apparently need in order to have that (some?) claims true on the aims analysis are true on the standards analysis is the following:

Every true ultimate claim is a true base prescriptive claim.

2. Does true by virtue of standards imply true by virtue of aims?

Example 108   (Example 30 again)

Dick: We shouldn't leave the lights on when we're away.

Zoe: Why?

Dick: Because we should do all we can to conserve energy.

Analysis   The following inference supplemented by some obvious descriptive claims is valid given the circumstances:

(a)   We do all we can to conserve energy.

Therefore, we do not leave the lights on when we're away.

So by the Basic Rule, if "We should do all we can to conserve energy" is plausible, then it follows that "We shouldn't leave the lights on when we're away" is plausible, where "shouldn't" is taken in the sense of refraining.

If Dick and Zoe accept that "We should do all we can to conserve energy" is plausible, it seems that they have the aim "To do all we can to conserve energy." Not leaving the lights on when they're away won't completely fulfill that aim, but it is better than the alternative of leaving the lights on or not doing anything, which amounts to not paying any attention to whether the lights are on. It's easy to turn off the lights. So "We shouldn't leave the lights on when we're away" is true.

The example suggests that we need the following:

If "You should do Y" is true on the standards approach,
then "Do Y" is a good/acceptable aim.

But the standards approach does not discriminate between personal, interpersonal, and impersonal justifications of prescriptive claims.

We could require that base prescriptive claims be classified as personal, interpersonal, or impersonal in terms of the kinds of justification they have in the standards approach. We can't describe that in a general way because there are too many different kinds of justifications people have proposed for accepting base prescriptive claims. Assuming a classification of base prescriptive claims, the classification could then be extended to all prescriptive claims by saying that if A is deducible from B, C, D, . . . then A is afforded the least classification that any of those claims have, where we rank personal below interpersonal and interpersonal below impersonal. Then, for example, for a non-base prescriptive claim to be personal, there is no deduction to it from only impersonal or interpersonal prescriptive claims. Thus, the classification scheme would be non-constructive. However, in the use of the scheme when going from the standards to the aims approach, we need only consider relevant to the analysis what the particular people believe about how the claim is classified.

Assuming that we have such a classification of prescriptive claims on the standards approach, and assuming that the classification is compatible with the way we use those terms in the truth-conditions on the aims analysis, it seems we need the following to go from the truth of claims on the standards approach to the truth of claims on the aims approach.

> *True base prescriptive claims yield good/acceptable ultimate aims*
> Every true base (personal/interpersonal/impersonal) prescriptive claim yields a good/acceptable (personal/interpersonal/impersonal) ultimate aim.

What about claims that are not base?

Example 109 (Compare the previous example)
Dick: (a) We should install photoelectric panels to connect in with the electric grid.
Zoe: Why?
Dick: (b) Because we should do all we can to conserve energy.

Analysis It's hard and expensive to install photoelectric panels compared to many other options for achieving the aim of conserving energy. So it seems that on the aims approach (a) is false.

But Zoe, reasoning by the standards approach, will also say that (a) doesn't follow from (b). That's because of the clause "all we can." In this example, the strength of the inference from (b) to (a) is a measure of how hard it is to do (a).

Example 110 (Compare Example 32)
(a) Smoking destroys people's health.
(b) We should tax activities that are destructive of people's health.
So (c) We ought to raise the tax on cigarettes.

Analysis By virtue of (a), (c) follows from (b). But (b) is implausible. We should tax people biting their toenails? We should tax mountain climbing?

As we adjust the standard (b) to make it more plausible, we will get that "We should raise the tax on cigarettes" follows from a more plausible standard. We are, in essence, putting a version of the clause "that we can" in the last example into the standard. Once we have that, then it seems that given our earlier assumptions, we'll have (c) on the aims approach, too.

Suppose that "You do X" is some general claim of which "You do Y" is a particular, as in the examples above. Then since doing Y is a part of doing X in the sense of being a particular that is inferred from the general, doing Y is better than doing nothing towards fulfilling "Do X." The only options that will do more towards fulfilling "Do X" are doing more particulars of the general "You do X," which will be harder. The only question remaining is whether doing Y is the easiest way to accomplish "Do X" at least in part. And that, as suggested in the last two examples, will be true to the degree that the standard "You should do X" is plausible in terms of doing "all you can."

There is no simple way to go from the truth of a prescriptive claim on the standards approach to the truth of that claim on the aims approach. To have any general way requires that not only the methods of justification of base prescriptive claims be compatible with the aims approach but that the methods of deduction and plausibility we use on the standards approach correlate well to the condition we impose on doing something being the best option for achieving an aim.

This concludes my attempt to understand better how to reason with prescriptive claims. We have two approaches, each sufficiently general to accommodate many different metaphysics, and we have some idea of how those approaches relate. But even if we understand these quite well, we will understand better only how to reason about what should be done. What should be done—what are our most fundamental prescriptions and aims—is a question beyond logic.

Appendix   Other Analyses of Reasoning with Prescriptive Claims

1. A logic of commands

Some say that what I call "prescriptive claims" are not claims at all. Such utterances are really commands or suggestions, and we should develop a logic of commands distinct from reasoning with claims. The problem then is how to integrate a logic of commands with a logic of descriptive claims in order to have a notion of inference that encompasses both. The work in Section A is meant to show that we can accomplish such an integration by assimilating good advice to truth, using conversions of imperatives or infinitives into descriptive claims when needed.[24]

2. Coherence

The standards approach to analyzing prescriptive claims is foundationalist. Certain standards are taken as basic, and from those by arguments—not just inferences—we derive further true prescriptive claims.

The aims approach too is foundationalist. Certain aims are ultimate and determine in part which prescriptive claims are true.

A different approach is to say that there is no "right" place to start. What is important is only how a particular collection of prescriptive claims "coheres."

Coherence is invariably said to require consistency: the claim A does not cohere with B, C, D, . . . if together they do not make a consistent collection of claims. But then we ask what notion of consistency is intended. Invariably a particular logic is invoked, typically classical predicate logic, but the same problem arises with any other logic. Then we must ask why we should adopt that logic as our standard. Every logic is either explicitly or implicitly based on some semantic analysis of propositions. Such assumptions are needed to give a justification of both the propositions taken as axiomatic in the logic and the methods of inference allowed in the logic. But we cannot fall back on coherence for justifying the logic because we need the logic to define coherence.

It seems that the coherentist view of prescriptive claims assumes a greater value for consistency in reasoning than for any other prescriptive judgment but gives no justification for that, or at least the coherentist does not build on semantic assumptions necessary for that in order to give a semantic analysis of prescriptive claims.

A bigger problem for the coherentist is how to distinguish a good coherent collection of claims from a bad one, or a better one from a less acceptable one. Some outside standard is needed. In "Prescriptive Theories?" in this volume I discuss the idea that the claims should best reflect our intuition about what is acceptable.

3. "Should" as a modal operator

Some have suggested that we understand prescriptive claims along the lines of alethic modalities.

Alethic modal logic is a formal analysis of the notions of necessity and possibility. Modal operators are used, so "It is necessary that dogs kill cats" is read as "Necessarily (dogs kill cats)," and "It is possible that dogs kill cats" is read as "Possibly (dogs kill cats)." The equivalence of "Possibly A" and "Not: Necessarily (Not A)" is taken as fundamental.[25]

Similarly, it is proposed that we take "should" as a modal operator. Thus, "Dogs should kill cats" becomes "Should (dogs kill cats)." In addition, "Allowed" is taken as a modal operator, and "Allowed A" is taken to be equivalent to "Not: Should (Not A)." This approach contrasts with the development in this paper where I have taken "You should do X" as atomic. By treating "should" as a modal operator, it's said, the formal methods of alethic modal logic can be used as a pattern or basis for the development of a logic. Possible worlds can be used to explain how to reason with alethic modalities; and if something like that could be devised for prescriptive modalities, we would have a ready-made analysis of great depth.

With alethic modalities, the question arises whether understanding those as operators involves a use-mention confusion. This issue shows up when we try to iterate modalities. "Necessarily (Necessarily (Dick is a human being))" is difficult to understand; it seems to require the reading "It is necessarily true that it is necessarily true that Dick is a human being." The "is true" part shows that the "that"-operator is at best a suspect disquotational device. The analysis of the claim in a formal modal logic, however, is pointed to as a clear way to understand such a sentence. Thus, it's said, the use-mention problem either evaporates or is harmless.

But consider "Should (should (Dick takes out the trash))." Who is the person to whom this prescription is made? We no longer have a subject. We can't unpack it as "Dick should Dick should take out the trash," but only as, perhaps, "It should be the case that Dick should take out the trash." The latter would have to be a truly impersonal "should"-claim, which is quite at odds with the intuitions about prescriptions we've built on here. We might require that each prescriptive modal operator requires a subject, so an iterated prescriptive modal claim would be "Should (Zoe should (Dick takes out the trash))" corresponding to "Zoe should ensure that Dick should take out the trash." If a formal modal logic analysis could give a clear reading of that, how could we judge if that reading is correct absent some intuition of what the sentence means? What can Zoe do to ensure that Dick should take out the trash? Either Dick should take out the trash or he shouldn't. Zoe yelling at him might ensure that he believes he should take out the trash, but that isn't the same as ensuring that "Dick should take out the trash" is true. If we can't make sense of iterated prescriptive modalities, one of the principal motives for developing a formal modal prescriptive logic is gone.[26]

Assuming, though, that questions of use-mention and iteration of modalities can be resolved, we have the problem of what in the mechanism of the semantics of a formal modal prescriptive logic could play the role of possibilities and relations between possibilities in the semantics of formal alethic modal logics. Possibilities arise naturally in our ordinary understanding of inferences and of claims like "It is possible that Dick took out the trash." For claims such as "Dick should take out the trash" it is suggested that "permissible states of affairs" are what should be considered, that is, possibilities in which certain prescriptive claims are taken as true. A relation between such sates of affairs is needed for the mechanism of the modal logic: one state is permissible relative to another if no obligation that is true in the first is not also true in the second.

But then an important motive for developing a prescriptive modal logic is lost. A key axiom of formal alethic modal logics that allows clear and simple semantics is:

If Necessarily (A), then A.

This axiom is uncontroversial: if it's necessary that a claim is true, then the claim really is true. But the comparable claim for prescriptive modalities is false:

If Should (A), then A.

Zoe may hope that it's true, but "If Dick should take out the trash, then Dick takes out the trash" is, as she and he well know, false.

Still, there has been considerable development of such modal approaches to reasoning with prescriptive claims in which these problems are said to be overcome.[27] But none of those can be satisfactory as a guide to reasoning with prescriptive claims because they are designed to investigate reasoning that discriminates only between valid and invalid inferences. As we have seen, we use and need to use in our ordinary reasoning strong as well as valid inferences. No one has shown how to modify formal alethic modal logics to deal with strong as well as valid inferences, and it would seem just as hard to do that for prescriptive modalities.

I am not saying that it is not possible to develop a modal logic approach to reasoning with prescriptive claims. But these problems suggest that such an approach is not promising, and work on it, under the name "deontic logic," has not resolved these problems.[28]

Notes

1. (p. 5) Alan R. White in *Truth*, Chapter 3.b, surveys arguments for and against this view and comes to a similar position:

> We often think of moral pronouncements as something which can not merely be agreed or disagreed with, argued about, or contradicted, but also as being about what can be discovered, assumed or proved, believed, doubted or known; all of which characterize what can be true or false. p. 61

2. (p. 7) See the many examples in *Critical Thinking*.

3. (p. 7) See my *Propositional Logics*.

4. (p. 8) See my *Propositional Logics*. In Chapter IX there I discuss some paraconsistent logics in which truth is taken as the default truth-value.

5. (p. 28) See "Base Claims" in *The Fundamentals of Argument Analysis*.

6. (p. 29) See "Arguments" in *The Fundamentals of Argument Analysis*.

7. (p. 31) For more on this comparison, see the quotations from Jonathan Dancy, on p. 147 in "Prescriptive Theories?" below.

8. (p. 35) David Hume, *A Treatise of Human Nature*, III, i, 1.

9. (p. 36) See James Rachels, "Naturalism."

10. (p. 36) See, for example, Jeff McMahan, "Moral Intuition," quoted in "Prescriptive Theories?" on pp. 148–151 below, and Philip L. Quinn, "Divine Command Theory." For the case of religious justification on this view, saying that "Killing cats is good" because Dog commands it isn't a reduction of the truth-value of that claim to a descriptive one, for one can further ask how one knows that Dog commands that, which, it seems, will eventually lead to invoking a religious revelation.

11. (p. 37) From "The Autonomy of Ethics." My analyses differ from his.

12. (p. 38) Max Black, "The Gap Between 'Is' and 'Should'."

13. (p. 49) In "Reasoning About Cause and Effect" in *Cause and Effect, Conditionals, Explanations*, I show that the standard examples that purport to show how cause and effect can be simultaneous are at best unconvincing.

14. (p. 54) Compare the discussion in Ruth Barcan Marcus, "Moral Dilemmas and Consistency."

15. (p. 54) Compare how this is done for the liar paradox in my "A Theory of Truth Based on a Medieval Solution to the Liar Paradox" (evised as Chapter XXII of *Classical Mathematical Logic*).

16. (p. 55) Bas C. Van Fraassen, "Values and the Heart's Command," p. 9.

17. (p. 58) Compare Kurt Baier in *The Moral Point of View: A Rational Basis of Ethics* (as quoted in *Value and Obligation*, ed. Richard B. Brandt, Harcourt, Brace & World, Inc., 1961, p. 134):

> Consider an example. Count O. believes his wife to have been unfaithful to him with Casanova. He believes he ought to kill both Casanova and the Countess. In fact, however, she has not been unfaithful to him and, therefore, he really ought not to kill either Casanova or the Countess. What, then, ought he to do? What he *thinks* he ought, "his subjective duty"? Or what he *really* ought, "his objective duty"?
>
> The paradox disappears as soon as we remember that, in deliberation, the agent has to accomplish a theoretical and practical task and that, in evaluating the agent's performance, we can criticize him on two quite different grounds, the inadequate performance either of his theoretical task or of his practical task. When this distinction is drawn, the paradoxical question vanishes. For all that we can in reason demand of the *agent* is that he should first complete, to the best of his ability, his theoretical task *and then act in accordance with* whatever answer he has arrived at in completing that task. The agent, therefore, can never ask himself, "Should I do what I *think* best or what *is* best?" For his theoretical task is to find out, to the best of his ability, what *is* best. The completion of his task will be what he thinks best. He cannot *at the same time think another course of action to be the best*. Count O. can think either that killing Casanova and his wife is best *or* that something else is best. He cannot think that killing Casanova and his wife is what he *thinks* best and at the same time that not killing anybody *really* is the best. In the course of deliberation, only the question What is the best action? can arise. Thus, for the agent the paradoxical question is impossible.

18. (p. 64) The terms "prescriptive" and "normative" are often used interchangeably. But these examples suggest that "normative" is inappropriate except when the norms are interpersonal or impersonal.

19. (p. 73) Compare David Schmidtz in *Rational Choice and Moral Agency*, pp. 12-13:

> Sometimes, at least, we call a choice rational because we think it will serve the chooser's ends. Understood in this way, to call a choice rational is, first, to endorse it, second, to have a reason for endorsement, and third, to have as one's reason for endorsement that the choice will serve the

chooser's ends.* When I call a choice rational, I may be saying that it will in fact serve the chooser's ends or that the chooser has good reason to think it will (whether or not it actually does so). In any case, rational choice, as understood here, involves seeking to choose effective means to one's ends. This is the heart or my characterization of rational choice.

* [Footnote] What do we mean when we call a *person* rational? We are endorsing the person neither as a means to the person's ends nor as a means to someone else's ends. Typically we are saying that the person is using his or her cognitive capacities in a way that effectively serves his or her ends. Similarly, to call a choice rational is to endorse it as a means to the chooser's ends, but such endorsement implies an assumption that the choice involved deliberation. Otherwise, the endorsement is not apt.

20. (p. 73) These debates are summarized by Gerd Gigerenzer in "Bounded andRational." See the discussion of the economist's notion of rationality in my "On Models and Theories" in *Reasoning in Science and Mathematics* in this series.

21. (p. 73) See, for example, the papers in *The Blackwell Guide to Ethical Theory*, ed. Hugh LaFollette.

22. (p. 74) For example, Spinoza, *Ethics*, Part 3, Proposition 9, says:
From what has been said it is plain, therefore, that we neither strive for, wish, seek, nor desire anything because we think it to be good, but, on the contrary, we ajudge a thing to be good because we strive for, wish, seek, or desire it.

23. (p. 77) This discussion is not meant to be an accurate exposition of Kant's views or of those working in the tradition he started but only a suggestion of a comparison of that tradition to the analyses here.

24. (p. 93) Peter B. M. Vranas in "New Foundations for Imperative Logic I: Logical Connectives, Consistency, and Quantifiers," suggests something like a three-valued approach for truth and satisfiability of descriptive and prescriptive claims. That paper also contains references and discussion of work on developing a logic of commands.

25. (p. 94) See Chapter V of my *Propositional Logics* for a presentation of formal logics of alethic modalities, an overview of which is given in "Conditionals" in *Cause and Effect, Conditionals, Explanations* in this series.

26. (p. 95) See Arthur N. Prior, "Logic, Deontic" or Lennart Åqvist, "Deonitic Logic" for the ideas behind this approach and analyses of these difficulties.
    John Horty in "Agency and Deontic Logic" builds "agency" into a formal modal logic analysis of prescriptions.

27. (p. 95) See, for example, Paul McNamara's survey "Deontic Logic."

28. (p. 95) Alan Ross Anderson in "A Reduction of Deontic Logic to Alethic Modal Logic," proposes a way to define deontic logics within any normal modal logic.

> Let "*P*" describe some "bad" state-of-affairs (either, on a teleological ethical theory, "bad" because of its consequences, or on a deontological theory, "bad" inherently). Then to say that *p* is obligatory is to say that failure of *p* leads to a state-of-affairs *P* which is "bad", but avoidable ($\Diamond \neg P$); and to say that *p* is forbidden is to say that *p* itself leads to the bad but avoidable state-of-affairs. p. 103

That is, "It is *obligatory* that *p*" is defined as: $\Box$ ($\neg p \supset P$). This approach allows for modeling different views, depending on what one takes as *P*. At first glance, it looks like it will give a completely impersonal analysis, but *P* could be personal. However, it is not applicable to reasoning with strong inferences. Arthur Prior in "Logic, Deontic" discusses other criticisms of this approach.

Truth and Reasoning

A major goal of reasoning is to establish truths and to determine what would follow if certain assumptions are true. There are many different notions of what is true, both in what kinds of things are true or false and what makes them true or false. By looking at what is common to those, we can find an idea of truth and the things that are true that can accommodate many particular views of truth and account for the wide agreement on what counts as good reasoning.

What kind of things are true or false?

We reason to try to determine what is true and what is false. We reason to try to determine what would be true if certain assumptions are true. We learn to reason as we learn our language. We reason together so we can reason alone. Reasoning is a kind of communication.

To reason well we need to understand the nature of truth and falsity and how those classifications function in our reasoning. To begin, let's consider what kind of things are true or false. When we reason together, we use language. We make sounds or write inscriptions. Or, reasoning with ourselves, we imagine a sound or inscription.[1]

Whether we view such utterances and inscriptions as true or false, or whether we think it's the meaning of such language that's true or false, or whether we think such language points to an abstract realm

of things that are true or false, it's through our use of language that
we reason. So to begin, let's focus on such utterances and inscriptions.
Later we'll consider whether they only represent or point to what is
actually true or false.

What kinds of linguistic sounds and inscriptions are (or represent
what is) true or false? It could be just a word, as when looking out
the window I say to a friend, "Raining." It could be as complex as a
sentence that takes half a page. It could be an equation composed of
mathematical symbols.

We can, however, exclude questions, commands, and wishes. We
can also exclude sounds that are nonsense, such as "Frabjous day," or
apparently good language that is really meaningless, such as "7 is
divisible by light bulbs." We can exclude ambiguous utterances, such
as "I am half-seated," and ones that are too vague, such as "America is
a free country."

It would seem, then, that for a piece of language to be a candidate
for being true or false, it must be completely precise and intelligible.
But if only language that is completely precise can be true or false,
then "Strawberries are red" does not qualify. Which strawberries?
What hue of red? Measured by what instrument or person? So we
couldn't analyze:

($\ddagger$) If strawberries are red, then some colorblind people cannot see
          strawberries among their leaves.
     Strawberries are red.
     Therefore: Some colorblind people cannot see strawberries
          among their leaves.

This is an example of acceptable reasoning, reasoning that any rules we
devise about how to reason well must be able to account for.[2] Yet any
attempt to make the language in ($\ddagger$) fully precise will fail. At best we
can redefine terms, using others that may be less vague.

No two people have identical perceptions, and since the way we
understand words depends on our experience, we all understand words
a little differently.[3] There has to be some wiggle room in the meaning
of what we say for us to be able to communicate. When Zoe says,
"Spot's barking woke Dick" (she was up late working on her term
paper when Spot started yelping), is that true or false? The language
is not too vague, unless we need, for some reason, some purpose,
more precision. When did Spot begin to bark? When exactly did

Dick awake? How long did Spot bark? How loud? What kind of yelping or howling or growling or ferocious arfing was it? "Oh, that doesn't matter," says Zoe, "you know very well what I mean." The issue isn't whether a sentence or piece of language is vague but whether it is *too vague*, given the context, for us to be justified in saying it's true or false.

Our goal is to have complete clarity in our reasoning. But that is and can only be a goal. What we take to be true or false must depend to some extent on our purposes, on what we pay attention to. Every description of the world of our experience is at best partial. We are limited in our descriptions by the resources of our language, by the resources of our sensory apparatus (how do dogs smell so much?), by how we process the experiences of our senses, and by how much of what we process we pay attention to. Do we choose to pay attention to only part of our experience? Psychologists will tell us no, yet we have available to us more than we first note. A clock striking four o'clock may not register as four to us; but if asked to recall, often we can say, "One, two, three, four. Yes, it struck four times."

Meaning does not reside in a piece of language; it does not reside in us; it does not reside in the world. It resides in us, language, and the world—in us using language to talk about the world and our experience. Meaning is in a particular use of language, in a particular context, among particular people. Meaning is not fixed, not for us individually and most certainly not among ourselves when we talk. We have to negotiate meaning.

We negotiate meaning to try to understand each other better, or perhaps at all. I, you negotiate meaning with ourselves each time we use language in a different way, or in a different context, or just when we reflect on what we say. We negotiate meaning with others, trying to fix more closely how we understand what we say so that we can have some confidence that we are communicating, that we understand together. The need for such negotiation may be evident only from our actions and disagreements. When we negotiate meaning with ourselves, we may do no more than think about what we are saying.

Whether we accept a piece of language as a candidate for being (what represents what is) true or false depends on our purposes, which we may negotiate as we negotiate meaning. What we pay attention to may be culture-bound by the resources of our language and by what we deem important in our experience, which is often codified by our language. But once given that framework in which to deal with our experiences, truth need not be relative.

"No, Spot's barking didn't wake Dick since he was stirring and coughing before Spot started to bark." We can claim evidence. We can compare experiences within our framework. But no framework is available to us to judge all of what there is, for we are limited. And thank Dog for that, for what horror to perceive all undiluted, to register all we perceive, to put into language all we have registered.

Perhaps there is a real framework in which to judge truth and falsity, in which to judge all. Perhaps God, or the gods, or Dog who smells all can perceive such a framework. Perhaps we can or should hold up such a framework as what we strive to see. But we are investigating how to reason well, and our limitations cannot be ignored.

So it is sufficient for our purposes in reasoning to ask whether we can agree that a particular piece of language, or class of inscriptions as in a formal language, is suitable to assume to be true or false, that is, to have a truth-value. If we cannot agree that a particular sentence such as "The King of France is bald" has a truth-value, then we cannot reason together using it. That does not mean that we employ different methods of reasoning or that all reasoning is psychological; it only means that we differ on certain cases. The assumption that we agree that a piece of language has a truth-value, that the imprecision of it is inessential, is always present, even if not explicit.[4]

The words "agree" and "negotiate" are somewhat misleading. Almost all our agreements, conventions, assumptions are implicit, tacit. They needn't be conscious or voluntary. Many of them may be due to physiological, psychological, or perhaps metaphysical reasons; for the most part we don't and perhaps may never know. Agreements are manifested in lack of disagreement and in that we communicate. Agreements are the result of our negotiations which are often done tacitly, with no verbal assent or even talk. To be able to see that we have made, or been forced into, or simply have an agreement is to be challenged on it. If I say "Cats are nasty" and you disagree with me, then I know that you consider that utterance to be true or false.[5]

So I suggest that we begin with the following definition:

> A *claim* is a written or uttered piece of language that
> we agree to view as being either true or false.

When reasoning with ourselves, we might not write or utter anything. But such reasoning can be understood as dependent on how we reason with sounds and inscriptions, using our imagination to think of the claims.[6]

Perhaps it is these utterances and inscriptions that are true or false in the negotiations and agreements we have made. Perhaps it is the meanings of them that are true or false in the negotiations and agreements we have made. Perhaps these utterances and inscriptions only represent or point to some abstract things called propositions that are really true or false, the pointing being what we negotiate and come to agreements about. No matter. It is these we use when we reason together. So it is these we can discuss, leaving to the metaphysicians to clarify the grounds of our negotiations and agreements.

Example 1   I wish I could get a job.

Analysis   If Maria, who's been trying to get a job for three weeks, says this to herself late at night, then this isn't a claim. It's more like a prayer or an extended sigh.

But if Dick's parents are berating him for not getting a job, he might say, "It's not that I'm not trying. I wish I could get a job." That might be true, but it also might be false, so the example would be a claim.

It is not a sentence type or an inscription devoid of context that is a claim. A claim is a specific piece of language in a specific context.

Example 2   Wanda is fat.

Analysis   Wanda weighs 120 kgs and is 1.7m tall, so almost all of us would agree with this example. We take it to be a claim.

If Wanda were the same height yet weighed only 50 kgs, we'd all disagree with it, which shows that we'd take it to be a claim then, too.

But if she weighed 72 kgs, we'd be unsure. It isn't that we don't know what "fat" means; we just don't think the sentence is true of false. We don't classify it as a claim. It isn't that our notion of claim is vague; we're clear that we won't classify it as true or false. It's the sentence itself that is too vague in that context to classify as a claim.

But if there's no clear division between what we mean by someone being fat or not being fat, doesn't that mean that we don't have a clear notion of claim? No. That we cannot draw a line does not mean there is no obvious difference in the extremes.

Claims are types

Suppose we're having a discussion. An implicit assumption that underlies our talk is that we will continue to use words in the same way, or, if you prefer, that the meanings and references of the words we use won't vary. This assumption is so embedded in our use of language that it is hard to think of a word except as a representative of inscriptions that look the same and utterances that sound the same. I do not know how to make precise what I mean by "look the same" or "sound the same," but we know well enough in writing and conversation what it means for two inscriptions or utterances to be *equiform*. So we can make the following agreement.

Words are types   We assume that throughout any particular discussion equiform words have the same properties of interest to us for reasoning. We therefore identify them and treat them as the same word. Briefly, *a word is a type*.

Some say that types are abstract objects. We cannot point to a type, only to a representative of it, for example, "Ralph is a dog." But all that we use and need in our reasoning is a process of identification of utterances or inscriptions. The reason we make those identifications may be by our intuiting or having some non-sensory access to abstract objects called "types," or it may be due to our psychology, or physiology, or culture.

The assumption that words are types, in this sense, is an abstraction from experience, but it is also an agreement to limit ourselves. Though a useful abstraction, it rules out many sentences we can and do reason with quite well. For example, we shall have to distinguish the three equiform inscriptions in "Rose rose and picked a rose," using some device such as "$Rose_1$ $rose_2$ and picked a $rose_3$" or "$Rose_{name}$ $rose_{verb}$ and picked a $rose_{noun}$."

Now consider a simple piece of reasoning:

If Socrates was Athenian, then Socrates was Greek.
Socrates was Athenian. Therefore, ...

If claims are inscriptions, then the two equiform occurrences in this are distinct claims. How can we reason with them?

Since words are types, we can argue that the two equiform inscriptions here are both true or both false. It doesn't matter where they're placed on the paper, or who said them, or when they were uttered. Their properties for reasoning depend only on what words and punctuation appear in them in what order. Any property that differentiates them isn't of concern to reasoning. We can make the following agreement.

Claims are types In the course of any reasoning, we consider an uttered or written piece of language to be a claim only if any other piece of language that is written or uttered and that is composed of the same words in the same order with the same punctuation can be assumed to have the same properties of concern to our reasoning during that analysis. We therefore identify equiform inscriptions or utterances and treat them as the same claim. Briefly, *a claim is a type*.

Again, to say that we can make this agreement does not necessarily mean it is just a convention. I do not deny that there might be good reasons for our agreements, say, that there are abstract objects called "types of sentences" which, perhaps without our being aware, have led us to this agreement or at least justify the agreement as the only possible way to proceed in reasoning.

But more fruitfully, we can see the agreement that we identify distinct utterances or inscriptions as being the same for all our logical purposes as an abstraction from experience, which is all we need when we say that *Ralph is a dog* and **RALPH IS A DOG** are representatives of the same type. Utterances are loud or soft, spoken clearly or mumbled. Inscriptions are typed or handwritten, in blue ink or black or red, they are on this page or that page or on a computer display. We are ignoring certain aspects of our experience in order to simplify our reasoning. This is part of the general procedure of creating a model of how to reason well. It is important at every stage to note what abstracting we do. If we encounter problems, contradictions, or counterintuitive consequences of our work, we can go back and see if perhaps part of what we chose to ignore in our experience might matter in a particular context.

For example, consider:

box **R** → | The sentence in box **R** contains forty-seven letters.

The sentence in box **R** contains forty-seven letters.

The two sentence inscriptions are equiform: they contain the same words in the same order with the same punctuation. But they are different for our reasoning. One refers to itself, one does not. To test the truth of the one on top, we need to consider whether it itself contains forty-seven letters, but that's not the case with the lower one. There is a clear and perceptible difference for our reasoning that is obscured by identifying them. In this case, though, the difference doesn't seem to matter.

But now consider:

box **S** → | The sentence in box **S** is not true. |

The sentence in box **S** is not true.

The inscription in the box is an example of the liar paradox, which seems to be both true and false. The inscription below it is not a version of the liar paradox but refers to the one above. The differences between these equiform inscriptions matter.[7]

The division of true and false

What is true is not false; what is false is not true. The world is, and our language, if used correctly, does not describe both what is and what is not with the same words. If "Ralph is a dog" is true, it can't be false; if "Ralph is a dog" is false, it can't describe how the world really is.

This, we believe, is the nature of truth because we believe that there is a world external to us, parts of which we are trying to describe. The world is coherent, out there, and if we use language correctly, no claim can be both true and false.

But then what about the apparent claims we make in ethics? What in the world is there that could make "You should never kill a dog" true or false? Yes, there are two categories for such sentences: good/bad, or correct/ incorrect, or just/unjust, or assertible/unassertible, or . . . , yet those divisions are not into the true and false. But compare these examples.

Example 3 Physician: Don't smoke anymore.
          Matilda: O.K.

Analysis Suppose that Matilda then goes out and smokes a couple cigarettes. We'd say she is perverse, or stupid, or she just didn't follow the doctor's orders. There's no question of belief or truth.

Example 4 Physician: You shouldn't smoke anymore.
    Matilda: I agree.

Analysis Suppose again that Matilda goes out and smokes a couple cigarettes. In this case we think she can be charged with inconsistency (if she hasn't changed her mind). That's because Matilda's attitude about "You shouldn't smoke" is one of belief. The doctor is not commanding her; such a conversation would typically be preceded or followed by an attempt by the doctor to convince her that she shouldn't smoke. And belief is belief that something is true.[8]

Perhaps, though, what Matilda is asked to believe is that the prescriptive claim is good advice. But to say that "You should stop smoking" is good advice is just to say that you should stop smoking.

The word "true" is odd in that we get nothing new by ascribing it to a sentence. That's equally so for these other divisions. Compare:

"Dick is an American" is true.
Dick is an American.

"New York is in the United States" is assertible.
New York is in the United States.

"Ralph should stop smoking" is good advice.
Ralph should stop smoking.

It's only when surveying or analyzing the use of the notions of truth and falsity and constructing theories that the words "true" and "false" play a significant role. *The labels* "is assertible" *and* "is good advice," *just like* "is true," *are shorthand for the conditions we look for in evaluating whether to accept a claim.* If we have those conditions, we might as well assert the claim.[9] It may be a simplification, but if so it is a simplification of great utility to seize on the following similarities:

These are the conditions under which you are justified in believing the sentence ~~is true~~.

These are the conditions under which you are justified in believing the sentence ~~is assertible~~.

These are the conditions under which you are justified in believing the sentence ~~is good advice~~.

The resistance to viewing various divisions we use in our reasoning as divisions into true and false follows, I suspect, from a particular metaphysics of truth and falsity: the true is what corresponds to the case, and that is independent of us and our interests. These other notions, it is said perjoratively, are dependent on our human capacities and interests, so they can't really be the division into the true and false. That is one particular metaphysics, a metaphysics that is part of a view of reasoning in which human capacities and interests are not considered constraints on models of good reasoning and the search for truth.

The divisions are dichotomies

The idea that what is true is not false, what is false is not true seems not only apt but obvious when we think of truth in terms of some kind of correspondence with a world external to us. But why should divisions into correct/incorrect, good/bad, ethical/unethical be mutually exclusive? Why can't we have a claim that is both ethical and unethical, or one that is good advice and not good advice, or one that is assertible and not assertible? The nature of our personal evaluations doesn't seem to rule that out.

Personal evaluations, at least of the type that give rise to a true/false division, are implicitly if not explicitly prescriptive. If it is good advice, you should do it; if it is bad advice, you shouldn't do it. If it is correct, then you should do it that way; if it is incorrect, then you shouldn't do it that way. If it is good, you should approve of it; if it is bad, you should disapprove. If a claim such as "You should never torture a dog" is both good advice/ethical/correct and bad advice/unethical/incorrect, then we are enjoined to both do and not do, to act and to act in a contrary manner. This we cannot do.

The *law of excluded middle* (every claim is true or false) and the *law of non-contradiction* (no claim is both true and false) are called "laws" by some because those principles lie at the heart of their metaphysics. But we can just as well see them as rules to simplify our reasoning. Or we can see them as reflecting a human capacity or need to classify as either-or. We adopt them as the basis of all our divisions into the true and false. We take each such division to be a dichotomy.

Even those who propose systems of reasoning based on the idea that there are degrees of truth, where a strict division is denied, still impose a division: a line is drawn that says on this side are claims we can use to derive further claims on which we can rely, the ones with "designated" values, the assertible ones, while on the other side are claims with undesignated values.[10] Between affirming and denying there seems to be no third choice.

But then what do we do in reasoning with a claim such as "You should never kill" when we find we have as good reason to believe it is true as to believe that it is false? We suspend judgment. But what if there is nothing more that could determine which it is: true or false?

We agree to view the sentence as a claim in order to determine whether it is true or whether it is false. But in doing so, we may find that the truth-conditions for it are indeterminate. We cannot then say that the sentence is both true and false without abandoning all our methods of reasoning, including those that led us to that conclusion. So we no longer agree to view the sentence as true or false but not both. We no longer take the sentence to be a claim.

Thus, physicists reasoned with "The ether has no mass" only to find that since there was no ether the sentence was neither true nor false, and so we no longer accept the sentence as a claim. We take the sentence "This sentence is false" to be a claim and in reasoning with it find that if it is true then it is false, and if it is false then it is true. We reason with it on the assumption that it is a claim in order to find that it is neither true nor false, and then no longer accept it as a claim.

So let us revise our definition of "claim."

Claims   A claim is a written or uttered piece of language that we agree to view as being either true or false but not both.

It is because we take these divisions to be dichotomies that we can devise methods of how to reason across a variety of subjects and purposes. These divisions function the same in our reasoning. The notions of possibility, inference, valid inference, and strong inference are all defined relative to the true/false division as a dichotomy, and all have been defined relative to both subjective as well as objective divisions.[11] I have shown how this is so for formal systems of reasoning in *Propositional Logics*. And in this series of books, *Essays on Logic as the Art of Reasoning Well*, I have used such dichotomies to establish rules for reasoning with arguments, explanations, mathematical proofs, reasoning in the sciences, conditionals, subjective claims, and prescriptive claims.

The false is what is not true

Given a dichotomy that functions as true and false in our reasoning, we have to ask whether certain utterances that appear to be claims but are stupid, or senseless, or bad, or worthless (depending on the particular notion we're investigating) should be classified as claims.

For example, "Green dreams jump peacefully" is a declarative sentence. But it doesn't make any sense. So without further qualification we have no motive to reason with it, and hence we don't take it to be a claim.

In contrast, when Suzy said to Dick "You should hold your breath for four minutes in order to stop hiccuping," we do indeed want to reason with the sentence. It's stupid, silly, but more, it's bad advice or wrong, so we classify it as false.

When someone says to us "The King of France is bald," it seems to be nonsense since there's no King of France. Yet that sentence might show up in our reasoning. It's stupid and wrong, but we can treat it as a claim, a false claim, for it certainly isn't true.

The problem of whether to jettison, to disregard sentences that are odd, or nonsensical, or too vague arises in a quite general way when we employ a formal language as a guide to the formation of propositions with which we'll reason. We carefully distinguish between syntax and semantics. The description of the formal language invokes no semantic aspects of the primitive parts of the language: we set out how to make well-formed-formulas solely in terms of structure and parts of speech. This division of form and content is invoked, usually implicitly, for every formal logic.[12] If we do not divide form and content, there are immense problems in specifying what counts as a sentence of the formal language and we cannot use the method of proof by induction on the form of formulas in analyzing the formal syntax and semantics.[13]

Once we have a formal language, we take certain linguistic expressions to realize the primitive symbols of the formal language, in the case of predicate logic both predicates and names (or linguistic expressions of those if you are a platonist). Then we have no choice, due to the division of form and content, but to say that every expression using these predicates and names that instantiates a formula of the formal language is meaningful and that every expression that instantiates a closed formula is a claim. That is, once we determine that the primitive parts of speech are meaningful, we commit ourselves to the entire stock of realizations of closed formulas as being not only meaningful but claims.

Suppose, then, that we take "is a dog" to be a predicate and the universe—the things we're reasoning about—to be all living animals. Suppose also that we take "Hubert" to be a name used to refer to a particular animal in that universe. And suppose that Hubert is a wolf-dog hybrid that eludes classification as either a dog or not a dog. Then "Hubert is a dog" is too vague to be taken as a proposition, yet we have agreed to accept it as one. In almost any realization of the formal language of predicate logic that we would wish to use as a guide to reasoning in our ordinary lives there will be sentences that we know are too vague to have a truth-value but which we are committed to treating as claims.

We can deal with such sentences that we would normally classify as nonsense or too vague to be claims by classifying them as false for the convenience of having a clear analysis of form distinct from meaning. Thus, the formalization of "The King of France is bald" is classified as false in predicate logic, and its negation is true. Thus, the formalization of "If the moon is made of green cheese, then $2 + 2 = 4$" is classified as false in relatedness propositional logic, and its negation as true. Thus, "Hubert is a dog" is classified as false, and so its negation is classified as true.

It may be a simplification to call such sentences true or false rather than senseless or stupid, but if so, it is a simplification of considerable utility. So we classify them as claims. But not as true claims. *They are false because they are not suitable to proceed on for deriving true claims.* This is how people treat all the notions that yield dichotomies that we take to be true-false divisions: *falsity is the default truth-value.* A claim must pass certain tests in order to be true; all other claims are classified as false, whether those tests are for assertibility, or for good advice, or for being sufficiently probable, or . . . .[14]

The problem of accommodating sentences that are nonsense or are too vague to be taken as claims into our stock of propositions when we use a formal logic is due to our attempt to give clear, usable models of reasoning. It is not a problem that is inherent in how to reason well but only in how to adopt a guide to how to reason well. The solution of it does not depend on nor illuminate our understanding of what is non-sense or a vague sentence. The solution is simply part of the apparatus, part of how we abstract from our experience in order to give a clear model. Only to the extent that we take conditions for a claim to be true as primary and falsity as the default truth-value can such a solution be said to reflect our deeper commitments to our notion of truth.

When is a claim true?

We say that "Dick likes chocolate ice cream" was true a year ago but is false today. But if that's really what we mean, then we have serious problems in saying how to reason with claims which can be true at one time and false at another. Better is to recognize that we are implicitly indexing the sentence with the time about which it is meant, so that there are two claims under discussion: "Dick liked chocolate ice cream a year ago" and "Dick likes chocolate ice cream today," the first of which is true and the second false. In such cases we can always mark a claim with the time it is meant to describe.

But now consider that Zoe said to Dick, "You should lose weight." If understood as meaning that losing weight will best achieve Dick's ends, then whether it is true or false is going to depend on Dick evaluating his various goals and how likely they are to be achieved or not achieved if he loses weight.[15] Dick's evaluations will change as he contemplates them, so it seems we can say that the claim is true or false only after Dick deliberates on it.

The problem of whether an utterance is a claim from the moment it is spoken or only after someone, or some group of people, or some creature makes an evaluation is endemic to all reasoning in which there is a subjective element. But it is a problem only if we adopt an attitude that there is an objective standard that a sentence must pass in order for it to be a claim: whatever conditions that determine whether it is true or false are satisfied or not at the moment the sentence is uttered. That standard seems not to be fulfilled in the claim about losing weight. But the adoption of that standard is also at issue.

Claims about the future have a similar problem. We all use and treat as a claim "It will rain tomorrow." Do we need to commit to the view that everything in the world is determined in advance for it to have a truth-value now?

The definition of "claim" is meant to avoid taking a stand on these issues. A sentence is a claim when we agree to view it as true or false. In all these cases it simplifies our reasoning enormously to view such sentences as true or false from the start of our consideration of them. If you wish, you can say that a proposition is what *is* true or false, and then what we are doing in our reasoning is establishing whether a particular sentence represents or correlates to a proposition. But then you're faced with explaining exactly what a proposition is, and how, if it is not the utterance in context, it can and does play a role in our reasoning. My sense is that invoking such propositions only serves to make it possible for those who want completely objective standards in their reasoning to have an object that is true or false, even when that object has no role other than marking a place we want to get to in our reasoning. More apt is to say that we reason with a sentence as if it is true or false in order to come to an evaluation of which it is, or to find that it is neither and hence not a claim.

Conclusion

We reason to arrive at truths. To do that we need to understand what we mean by saying that something is true or false.

Utterances or inscriptions that we call true or false are part of the experience of all of us in our reasoning. We can abstract from them to talk of types as true or false. In this way we can come up with a notion of claim that can be used in reasoning by people who take very different views of what kinds of things are true or false.

To say that an utterance is a claim is to agree to view it as true or false. That need not mean that it is true or false but only that we have some motive to treat it so, perhaps eventually finding that it is not suitable to be called true or false. That agreeing is often implicit, part of the general way we negotiate meaning.

The true/false division is often thought of as an objective classification of claims, corresponding in some way to how the world is. But there are many divisions we use in our reasoning that are based on what are apparently subjective evaluations. We can and do use divisions of utterances into good/bad, or acceptable/unacceptable, or assertible/unassertible, or right/wrong in the same way we use an objective notion of truth and falsity.

Those divisions are taken to be dichotomies: what is true is not false, and what is false is not true. Normally falsity is taken as the default truth-value so that we can accommodate odd or too-vague sentences into our reasoning.

In this way we have a general basis for reasoning that allows us to use the same methods across a wide variety of subjects and purposes.

Appendix 1   Are claims true or only represent what is true?

Claims are what we use in our reasoning. Some say, though, that what is true or false is not the utterance or inscription but the meaning or thought expressed by that, what they call a "proposition" or "mental proposition." So the following, if uttered at the same time and place, all express or stand for the same proposition:

(**) It's raining.
   Il pleut.
   Pada deszcz.
   Está chovendo.

The word "true," they say, can be properly applied only to things that cannot be seen, heard, or touched. Sentences "express" or "represent" or "participate in" such propositions.

Platonists take this one step further. A *platonist*, as I use the term, is someone who believes that there are abstract objects not perceptible to our senses which exist independently of us. Such objects can be perceived by us only through our intellect. The independence and timeless existence of such objects, they say, account for objectivity in reasoning and mathematics. In particular, propositions are abstract objects, and a proposition is true or is false, though not both, independently of our even knowing of its existence.

But the platonist, as well as the person who thinks a proposition is the meaning of a sentence or is a thought, reasons with language. For me to reason with someone who takes propositions to be what is true or false, it is not necessary that I believe in abstract objects or thoughts or meanings. It is enough that we agree that certain utterances and inscriptions are or from his viewpoint represent propositions. Whether such a piece of language expresses a true proposition or a false proposition is as doubtful to him as whether, from my view, it is true or it is false. The question of whether the four inscriptions at (**) express the same proposition for him amounts on my view to whether we should identify those four inscriptions for all our purposes in reasoning.

From my perspective, the platonist conception of logic is an idealization and abstraction from experience. From the platonist perspective, I mistake the effect for the cause, the world of becoming for the reality of abstract objects. But we can and do reason together using claims, and to that extent the definition of claim presented in this essay can serve platonists or those who hold other views of propositions. In analyzing any particular kind of reasoning, we can take those views into account as added weight to the significance of what we take to be true or false.[16]

But platonists argue that taking claims as the basis of reasoning is hopeless. They say we cannot answer precisely the questions: What is a sentence? What constitutes a use of a sentence? When has a sentence been used assertively or even put forward for discussion? These, they say, can and should be avoided by taking things inflexible, rigid, timeless as propositions. But that only pushes back these problems to: How do we use logic? What is the relation of these theories of abstract objects to our arguments, discussions, and search for truth? How can we tell if this utterance expresses that abstract proposition? It's not that taking claims to be true or false brings up questions that can be avoided. The emphasis on precision and objective standards in reasoning has gone too far if we cannot relate our work to its intended use as a guide to reasoning well.

In contrast to platonists, some say that mental propositions, what might be called thoughts, are what are true or false. Alexander Broadie describes a medieval view of that and, from what I can gather, his own view in *Introduction to Medieval Logic*:[17]

> That we use the sounds or marks we do use in order to communicate is not a fact of our nature, for we could have used other signs, and other nations do use other signs. But what I think of when I think of what I call a "man" is the same as what a Frenchman thinks of when he thinks of an "homme", and as what a Greek thinks of when he thinks of an "anthropos". The thought is the same though the conventional expression of it differs. Thus the language of thought is universal in contrast to what we may term the "parochiality" of conventional languages. Indeed the intertranslatability of conventional languages is due precisely to the fact that, different as they are in respect of many of their characteristics, they can all be used to express the same set of thoughts.   p. 8

This is an example of the triumph of hope over experience. We all hope, desperately, to be understood by others. We do not want to think that we are so separate that no one can see the world as we do. We only need to make the effort, perhaps a great effort, to phrase our thoughts well and others will understand exactly what we are thinking. But every day in every conversation, we have evidence that others do not understand as we do, that the thought we wished to convey is not what the other person understood by what we said. Approximately sometimes, but exactly most certainly not. This is one of the most obvious and clearest conclusions we can make from our experience of "communicating" with others. Yet we persist in believing that others have the same thoughts as we do. Anyone who knows well two languages will, on reflection, admit that there is no real inter-translatability between them but only some approximation. Much is lost in translation: *traduire c'est trahir.* What is maintained is, roughly, something like the truth-conditions of sentences, and even that only approximately.

We are not sure what thoughts are, even for ourselves. We know that they needn't be linguistic (gestures as well as pictures in our minds). But what exactly they are, when we have had one, what distinguishes one from another, this we cannot say. How, then, can we proclaim that others have the same thoughts we do? We don't even know when we have the same thought we had an hour ago.

It is hard to see how the truth or falsity of our thoughts could be the basis for an analysis of how to reason well.

Appendix 2   Coherence rather than truth

Some say that we should abandon the view that what is true is what corresponds to the case, no matter how that might be interpreted. Claims are true or false, they say, as they cohere with other claims in our general understanding of the world.[18]

Coherence is invariably said to require consistency: the claim A does not cohere with B, C, D, . . . if together they do not make a consistent collection of claims. But to invoke consistency is to invoke some methods of reasoning. On what basis should we accept those rules of reasoning? We would have no notion of validity, for that, too, depends on the notion of truth. We don't have any idea of what it means for a rule of inference to be acceptable if that isn't explained in terms of validity. We don't have any notion of what it means to take a claim as axiomatic, such as "Dogs are mammals or dogs are not mammals," unless we invoke the notion of tautology, which depends on a notion of truth. The whole enterprise of substituting coherence for truth is a sleight of hand, trying to divert our attention from the reliance on an informal, intuitive notion of truth to focus only on syntax. To say, for example, that "A or not A" is a fundamental principle that other principles have to cohere with, and we know this because, say, people use it that way, is to pretend that we can avoid all the hard work of trying to understand why we use that principle, what assumptions lie behind it, in favor of the superficial syntax. No reason is apparent even for why consistency should be demanded.

Appendix 3   Waismann on objective standards and the law of excluded middle

Many have written on the issues I discuss in this essay, too many to cite here. But one scholar, Friedrich Waismann, has discussed these issues in a way that particularly illuminates the analyses I have given.

In this first long extract from "Verifiability" (pp. 57–58) he discusses the interplay between convention and objective standards.

> Suppose there is a tribe whose members count "one, two, three, a few, many". Suppose a man of this tribe looking at a flock of birds said "A few birds" whereas I should say "Five birds",—is it the same

fact for him as it is for me? If in such a case I pass to a language of a different structure, I can no longer describe "the same" fact, but only another one more or less resembling the first. What, then, is the objective reality supposed to be described by language?

What rebels in us against such a suggestion is the feeling that the fact is there objectively no matter in which way we render it. I perceive something that exists and put it into words. From this it seems to follow that fact is something that exists independent of and prior to language; language merely serves the end of communication. What we are liable to overlook here is that the way we see a fact— i.e., what we emphasize and what we disregard—is *our* work. "The sun beams trembling on the floating tides" (Pope). Here a fact is something that emerges out from, and takes shape against a background. The background may be, e.g., my visual field; something that rouses my attention detaches itself from this field, is brought into focus and apprehended linguistically; that is what we call a fact. A fact is noticed; and by being noticed it becomes a fact. "Was it then no fact before you noticed it?" It was, if I *could* have noticed it. In a language in which there is only the number series "one, two, three, a few, many", a fact such as "There are five birds" is imperceptible.

To make my meaning still clearer consider a language in which description does not take the form of sentences. Examples of such a description would be supplied by a map, a picture language, a film, the musical notation. A map, for instance, should not be taken as a conjunction of single statements each of which describes a separate fact. For what, would you say, is the contour of a fact? Where does the one end and the other begin? If we think of such types of description, we are no longer tempted to say that a country, or a story told in a film, or a melody must consist in "facts". Here we begin to see how confusing the idea is according to which the world is a cluster of facts—just as if it were a sort of mosaic made up of little coloured stones. Reality is undivided. What we may have in mind is perhaps that *language* contains units, viz. *sentences*. In describing reality, describing it in the form of sentences, we draw, as it were, lines through it, limit a part and call what corresponds with such a sentence a fact. In other words, language is the knife with which we cut out facts. (This account is simplified as it doesn't take notice of *false* statements.) When we pass to a symbolism of language that admits of no sentences, we are no more inclined to speak of facts.

... Just as we have to interpret a face, so we have to interpret reality. The elements of such an interpretation, without our being aware of it, are already present in language—for instance, in such moulds as the notion of thinghood, of causality, of number, or again in the way we render colour, etc.

Noticing a fact may be likened to seeing a face in a cloud, or a figure in an arrangement of dots, or suddenly becoming aware of the solution of a picture puzzle: one views a complex of elements as one, reads a sort of unity into it, etc. Language supplies us with a means of comprehending and categorizing; and different languages categorize differently.

"But surely noticing a face in a cloud is not inventing it?" Certainly not; only you might not have noticed it unless you had already had the experience of human faces somewhere else. Does this not throw a light on what constitutes the noticing of facts? I would not dream for a moment of saying that I *invent* them; I might, however, be unable to perceive them if I had not certain moulds of comprehension ready at hand. These forms I borrow from language. Language, then, *contributes to the formation and participates in the constitution* of a fact; which, of course, does not mean that it *produces* the fact.

E.H. Gombrich in *Art and Illusion* fleshes out this view of "facts" or "reality" in exploring psychological bases of representation. In "The World as Process" I show a greater dependence of our conception of "reality" on language than either of these authors.

In this second long extract from "How I See Philosophy" (pp. 8–10) Waismann discusses the law of excluded middle and sentences about the future.

This doubt has taken many different forms, one of which I shall single out for discussion—the question, namely, whether the law of excluded middle, when it refers to statements in the future tense, forces us into a sort of logical Predestination. A typical argument is this. If it is true now that I shall do a certain thing tomorrow, say, jump into the Thames, then no matter how fiercely I resist, strike out with hands and feet like a madman, when the day comes I cannot help jumping into the water; whereas, if this prediction is false now, then whatever efforts I may make, however many times I may nerve and brace myself, look down at the water and say to myself, "One, two, three—", it is impossible for me to spring. Yet that the prediction is either true or false is itself a necessary truth, asserted by the law of excluded middle. From this the startling consequence seems to follow that it is already now decided what I shall do tomorrow, that indeed the entire future is somehow fixed, logically preordained. Whatever I do and whichever way I decide, I am merely moving along lines clearly marked in advance which lead me towards my appointed lot. We are all, in fact, marionettes. If we are not prepared to swallow *that*, then—and there is a glimmer of hope in the "then"—there is an alternative open to us. We need only renounce the law of excluded middle for statements of this kind, and with it the validity of ordinary logic, and all will be well. Descriptions of what will happen are, at present, neither true nor false. (This sort of argument was actually propounded by Lukasiewicz in favour of a three-valued logic with "possible" as a third truth-value alongside "true" and "false".)

The way out is clear enough. The asker of the question has fallen into the error of so many philosophers: of giving an answer before stopping to ask the question. For is he clear what he is asking? He seems to suppose that a statement referring to an event in the future is at present undecided, neither true nor false, but that when the event happens the proposition enters into a sort of new state, that of being true. But how are we to figure the change from "undecided" to "true"? Is it sudden or gradual? At what moment does "it will rain tomorrow" begin to be true? When the first drop falls to the ground? And supposing that it will not rain, when will the statement begin to be false? Just at the end of the day, at 12 p.m. sharp? Supposing that the event *has* happened, then the statement *is* true, will it remain so for ever? If so, in what way? Does it remain uninterruptedly true, at every moment of day and night? Even if there were no one about to give it any thought? Or is it true only at the moments when it is being thought of? In that case, how long does it remain true? For the duration of the thought? We wouldn't know how to answer these questions; this is due not to any particular ignorance or stupidity on our part but to the fact that something has gone wrong with the words "true" and "false" applied here.

If I say, "It is true that I was in America", I am saying that I was in America and no more. That in uttering the words "It is true that—" I take responsibility upon myself is a different matter that does not concern the present argument. The point is that in making a statement prefaced by the words "It is true that" I do not *add* anything to the factual information I give you. *Saying* that something is true is not *making* it true: cf. the criminal lying in court, yet every time he is telling a lie protesting, his hand on his heart, that he is telling the truth.

What is characteristic of the use of the words "true" and "false" and what the pleader of logical determinism has failed to notice is this. "It is true" and "It is false", while they certainly have the force of asserting or denying, are not descriptive. Suppose that someone says, "It is true that the sun will rise tomorrow" all it means is that the sun will rise tomorrow: he is not regaling us with an extra-description of the trueness of what he says. But supposing that he were to say instead, "It is true *now* that the sun will rise tomorrow", this would boil down to something like "The sun will rise tomorrow now"; which is nonsense. To ask, as the puzzle-poser does, "Is it true or false *now* that such-and-such will happen in the future?" is not the sort of question to which an answer can be given: which *is* the answer.

Waismann uses here the redundancy of the use of the phrase "is true" in the cases he is concerned with. I invoke that redundancy in a different way, to assimilate various classifications of claims to the single division into the true ones and the false ones. In contrast, I evade the issue of the import of the law of excluded middle with a definition of "claim" that allows for but does not suppose an objective basis for the classification into the true and false.

Notes

1. (p. 101) Some talk of "practical reason" in which no language is involved. It is not clear that practical reason has anything to do with reasoning in which the goal is to arrive at truths. See the section on dispositional rationality in the essay "Rationality" in this volume.

There are also some who point to experiments with birds and animals to say that reasoning does not require language. See, for example, *The Animal Mind* by James L. Gould and Carol Grant Gould, especially pp. 174–177. If that should prove true, then this essay and my other works should be seen as investigating reasoning as confined to language only.

2. (p. 102) Gottlob Frege in "The Thought: A Logical Inquiry" apparently takes this to be an acceptable inference.

3. (p. 102) Some say that a sentence such as "$2 + 2 = 4$" is fully precise and we understand it without any recourse to experience. Indeed, that sentence has been taken as both the archetype and standard for what we should accomplish in clarifying all our reasoning. But I show how our understanding of that sentence does depend on experience in "Mathematics as the Art of Abstraction" in *Reasoning in Mathematics and Science* in this series, and that it, too, is to some extent vague.

More generally in "Models and Theories" in *Reasoning in Science and Mathematics* I show how scientific laws are not claims but only schema of claims until we attempt to apply them and in doing so say how the terms in them are meant to be understood. This is exactly how we resolve the ambiguity in example (‡): the sentences in it are not true but only true enough on application; the inference is a scheme, not a particular, until we apply it.

4. (p. 104) One colleague objected that some community might agree to view "All blue ideas are beautiful" as having a truth-value, yet that doesn't mean it is true or false. From our perspective those people either have a very different notion of truth than we do or they understand the words in that sentence differently than we do. So long as their notion of truth functions in the framework of reasoning I describe below, we have no reason *as logicians* to say that they have a faulty notion of truth. The situation would be the same as when a community adopts a "deviant" arithmetic, as I discuss in "Why are there so many logics?" in *Reasoning and Formal Logic* in this series. We respect the reasoning of others to try to understand them, rather than dismissing the reasoning because of our inability to see immediately what they are doing.

5. (p. 104) Compare what John Lyons says in *Introduction to Theoretical Linguistics*:

> We have no direct evidence about the understanding of utterances, only about *misunderstanding*—when something "goes wrong" in the

process of communication. If, for instance, we say to someone *bring me the red book that is on the table upstairs* and he brings us a book of a different colour, or a box, or goes off downstairs in search of the book, or does something totally unexpected, we might reasonably say that he has "misunderstood" the whole or some part of the utterance (other explanations are of course possible). If he does what is expected (goes off in the right direction and comes back with the right book) we might say that he has correctly understood the utterance. . . . Normal communication rests upon the assumption that we all "understand" words in the same way; this assumption breaks down from time to time, but otherwise "understanding" is taken for granted. Whether we have or have not the same "concepts" in our "minds" when we are talking to one another is a question that cannot be answered otherwise than in terms of the "use" we make of words in utterances. It would probably be true, but rather pointless, to say that everyone "understands" a particular word in a slightly different way. Semantics is concerned with accounting for the degree of uniformity in the "use" of language which makes normal communication possible.   p. 411

6. (p. 105) Compare Isaiah Berlin in "Verification":

A proposition [is] any sentence which conveys to someone that something is or is not the case. And this seems on the whole to accord with common usage.   p. 16

In my earlier writings I said that a claim is a declarative sentence *used in such a way* that it is true or false, in order to avoid engaging in this discussion of the nature of agreements. However, the example "Raining" above shows that what is true or false need not be a sentence. Worse, a declarative sentence is usually defined to be one that is true or false.

7. (p. 108) A resolution of the liar paradox that depends on distinguishing these is due to Jean Buridan, as translated and explained by George Hughes in *John Buridan on Self-Reference*. I've given a modern formalization of that in "A Theory of Truth Based on a Medieval Solution to the Liar Paradox" (revised in Chapter XXII of *Classical Mathematical Logic*.)

8. (p. 109) Alan R. White in *Truth*, Chapter 3.b, surveys arguments for and against the view that prescriptions are true or false and comes to a similar position:

We often think of moral pronouncements as something which can not merely be agreed or disagreed with, argued about, or contradicted, but also as being about what can be discovered, assumed or proved, believed, doubted or known; all of which characterize what can be true or false.   p. 61

9. (p. 109) Compare Michael Dummett, *Elements of Intuitionism* p. 371:

> It is evident that it is fundamental to the notion of an assertion that it be capable of being either correct or incorrect; and therefore, in so far as assertion is taken to be the primary mode of employment of sentences, it is fundamental to our whole understanding of language that sentences are capable of being true or false, where a sentence is true if an assertion could be correctly made by uttering it, and false if such an assertion would be incorrect.

10. (p. 111) See my *Propositional Logics*.

Timothy Smiley in his "Comment on 'Does many-valued logic have any use?' by D. Scott" says:

> The way to defend [the method of designating truth-values] is to read "true" for "designated". The method of defining logical consequence then needs no justification, for it now reads as saying that a proposition follows from others if and only if it is true whenever they are all true. What does need explaining is how there can be more than two truth-values. The answer is that propositions can be classified in other ways than as true or untrue, and by combining such a classification with the true/untrue one we in effect subdivide the true and untrue propositions into a larger number of types. For example, given any property ϕ of propositions, there are prima facie four possible types of proposition: true and ϕ, true and not ϕ, untrue and ϕ, untrue and not ϕ. If ϕ is unrelated to truth, like "obscene" or "having to do with geometry", all four types can exist and we get four truth-values, two being designated and two undesignated. If ϕ has any bearing on truth some of the types may be ruled out; e.g., if ϕ is (perhaps) "about the future" or "meaningless", the type "true and ψ" will be empty, leaving three truth-values of which just one is designated. One cannot foretell how the connectives will behave with respect to this or that classification of propositions, but to the extent that the types of compound propositions turn out to be functions of the types of their constituents, so we shall get a many-valued logic.
>
> pp. 86–87

11. (p. 111) A discussion of subjective and objective standards is given in "Subjective Claims" by Fred Kroon, William S. Robinson, and me in *The Fundamentals of Argument Analysis* in this series of books.

In *Truth as One and Many* Michael P. Lynch takes truth to be a structural notion, too. But he bases his work on what he calls "folk beliefs" about the nature of truth that are far different from what I take as fundamental here. Yet he cites no studies to show that those assumptions are commonly held. Arne Naess in *"Truth" as Conceived by Those Who Are Not Professional*

Philosophers debunks all the talk that philosophers make about what the common notion of truth is, about what ordinary folks believe. He does a sociological experiment, questioning people about their views, and shows that there is not only no unanimity but a huge variety of views of truth all held by a more or less equally small percentage of the people he surveyed. Cory D. Wright in "On the Functionalization of Pluralist Approaches to Truth" summarizes and discusses current debates about whether truth is univocal or pluralist as well as claims by Lynch and others about the structural nature of truth.

12. (p. 112) See my *Propositional Logics* and *Predicate Logic*.

13. (p. 112) See "On the Error in Frege's Proof" in *Reasoning and Formal Logic* in this series for an example.

14. (p. 113) This is so for not only the formal logics studied in *Propositional Logics* but also for informal methods and rules for reasoning well that are analyzed in my other works. It is also crucial in developing a formal method of reasoning with non-referring names and resolving the liar paradox, as I show in *Classical Mathematical Logic*.

   Some logicians, either because they believe that there are true contradictions, or because they believe that there are some claims that are both true and false, or because they wish to model how to reason in the presence of (possible) contradictions without collapsing all deductions into triviality, propose what are called *paraconsistent logics*. In those, it seems, truth is taken as the default truth-value with tests set out for a claim to be false. See, for example, Chapter IX of *Propositional Logics*. But I know of no such logic that has clear enough semantics to merit consideration as proposing a view of truth and falsity as opposed to formal methods to justify a deductive system. If such clear semantics can be given, then a mirror image of the view here would be needed. In "Paraconsistent Logics with Simple Semantics" I show that we need not take truth as the default truth-value in order to have clear and well-motivated semantics for a logic in which not all claims follow from a contradiction.

15. (p. 114) See "Reasoning with Prescriptive Claims" in this volume.

16. (p. 116) Whenever abstract propositions or thoughts or meanings are invoked as what are true or false, it is the sentences that "express" them that are pointed to as our access to them. For example, Gottlob Frege in "Negation" says:

> How, indeed, could a thought be dissolved? How could the inter-
> connexion of its parts be split up? The world of thoughts has a model
> in the world of sentences, expressions, words, signs. To the structure
> of the thought there corresponds the compounding of words into a

sentence; and here the order is in general not indifferent. To the dissolution or destruction of the thought there must accordingly correspond a tearing apart of the words, such as happens, e.g., if a sentence written on paper is cut up with scissors, so that on each scrap of paper there stands the expression for a part of a thought.   p. 123

See also Frege's "The Thought: A Logical Inquiry."

Colwyn Williamson in "Propositions and Abstract Propositions" reviews these and other views of what a proposition is from a viewpoint similar to mine.

17. (p. 117) Aristotle, *De Interpretatione*, 1 , spoke similarly:

Spoken words are the symbols of mental experience and written words are the symbols of spoken words. Just as all men have not the same writing, so all men have not the same speech sounds, but the mental experiences, which these directly symbolize, are the same for all, as also are those things of which our experiences are the images.

18. (p. 118) See "The Coherence Theory of Truth" by James O. Young for a survey and other criticisms of this view.

Prescriptive Theories?

What is the difference between descriptive theories and prescriptive theories? Unless we assume that prescriptive theories are about value-judgments that are not true or false, and hence adopt a new methods and justification for our reasoning, there seems to be no difference that would affect how we construct and evaluate theories.

Two kinds of theories?

There are, apparently, two kinds of theories: prescriptive and descriptive. How can we distinguish between them?

Prescriptions vs. descriptions

A descriptive theory says how the world is, was, or will be. A prescriptive theory says how the world should be. This seems to be a clear difference we can use to distinguish these kinds of theories.

Classical propositional logic contains no prescriptive claims, yet we all take it to be prescriptive. This is the right way to reason: you should reason in accord with these standards.

Physics and chemistry are prescriptive in the same way. If you accept the assumptions of the theory and the methods of reasoning we employ, then you should accept the conclusions.

But for physics and chemistry it is belief that is enjoined, a prescriptive standard of rationality. For logic or ethics the prescription is to act.

Yet an engineer takes physics to be prescriptive for actions, too: if I want the bridge to stand up, I should build in accord with the claims of physics. The claims of physics are not themselves prescriptive. The prescription, either of belief or of action, is added to the theory.

We take all theories to be prescriptive for rationality. Any further prescription is added to the theory and is part of that prescription of rationality: if you accept the assumptions of the theory and the methods of reasoning employed in it, then you should accept—and act on—the consequences of the theory.

Still, there are some theories that are prescriptive in a clear and different way. Some ethical theories include prescriptive claims: you should do this, you ought to do that.

But some ethical theories have no such prescriptive claims. They say rather "Torturing children is wrong" or "Stealing is not just." What is prescriptive is again added to the theory: you should not do what is wrong or unjust. The form of the claims in a theory is not a good guide to whether or how it is prescriptive. Whether a theory is prescriptive is relative to the purposes we have in constructing and using it.

Prescriptive theories are about judgmental claims
Perhaps we can distinguish prescriptive theories or models (I use the terms interchangeably) in terms of the kinds of claims they are meant to model.[1]

Descriptive theories are meant to describe the world. Judgments enter only in reasoning within the theory and in choosing the theory.

Prescriptive theories are "judgmental" in that they are meant to account for and give guidance about our judgments, for example, whether an action is good or bad, whether a decision is just or unjust, whether reasoning is correct or incorrect. But, as discussed in "Truth and Reasoning," all claims are to some extent vague or at least open to interpretation. So to evaluate any claim as true or false requires judgment.[2] To evaluate whether "The electron made this path in this cloud chamber" is true may, by the conventions of physics, require almost no judgment . To evaluate whether "Dogs bark" may require more judgment. To evaluate "Dick is unhappy" may require more judgment still. There is not a clear division between theories whose claims require judgment to evaluate compared to those that don't. There is a spectrum.

But perhaps the division works well enough at the extremes. Scientific theories require almost no judgment in evaluating their claims while ethical theories require a great deal. Perhaps sociological theories can't be easily classified on one side of the divide and not the other, but that doesn't mean we can't use the division for those other theories.

But it isn't that physics requires almost no judgment in evaluating its data. It's that we've agreed on how to interpret the data, how to make those evaluations. When new ideas enter into physics, new interpretations of the data come to the fore, and then, for awhile at least, the data for the theory seem to require just as much judgment as an ethical theory where we have no such clear agreement on how to evaluate the claims.

I can't see how to clearly distinguish some theories as judgmental, that is, being about claims that require substantial judgment to evaluate, and others as simply descriptive. Theories in physics and chemistry we say are not judgmental because the judgments that are involved are so generally agreed upon that we find it hard even to see them, while for ethical theories we do not have such strong agreement. To use the spectrum as a way to divide theories would entail that at some times physics is descriptive and at other times, when its methods are called into question, it is judgmental.

The body of data of descriptive theories is fixed while that of prescriptive theories is open to revision
The body of data of a scientific theory is fixed, and the theory has to agree with that. The body of data of a prescriptive theory is not fixed, is often inconsistent, and if the theory contradicts the data, then that need not count against the theory. Even though this difference may be only a matter of degree, it is a difference that is clear enough at the extremes to be a practical division.

We can all see that the sun revolves around the earth. That's part of the data that any astronomical theory has to account for. But our astronomical theories say:

The sun does not revolve around the earth.

We all recognize that this table is solid; that's part of the data that a physical theory has to account for. But physics tells us:

This table is not solid.

We do revise the data to fit a "descriptive" theory.

We do so by saying that the data we have to account for are only what seem to be. It seems that the sun revolves around the earth. It seems that this table is solid. Astronomy and physics can account for those claims by invoking further claims about our perceptual abilities.

An ethical theory might contradict "You should never kill any person" even though many of us would say that's clearly true and part of the data the theory should account for. But in this case, too, we can account for the theory contradicting the data by invoking claims about our perceptions and misconceptions. If you believe these assumptions of the theory (just like in physics), you'll see that you were wrong about that claim being true. You were misled by paying attention to too few examples, or reasoning badly, or . . . .

There is a difference between physics and ethical theories in how we deal with contradictions of the data, but it is not a difference in kind. It is a matter of degree. With "scientific" theories, ones in physics and chemistry and biology, a contradiction with what we take to be the data is initially counted against the theory because our body of data is taken to be fixed. To revise the data rather than the theory involves challenging very fundamental conceptions about the world. With an ethical theory, the body of data does not appear to be as fixed and we are more willing to revise it in light of a theory that we accept.

Everyone recognizes and uses the distinction between descriptive and prescriptive theories

One section of *Introduction to Theoretical Linguistics* by John Lyons is titled "Linguistics is a descriptive, not a prescriptive, science." He explains this in a way that we can all understand: traditional grammar says how you should speak and write, whereas modern linguistics describes languages without any normative element.

But traditional grammar—what is taught to schoolchildren and non-native speakers—is not a theory. Traditional grammars are rule books. There is no intention to devise assumptions from which some or all of the rules follow, no prescription of rationality comes with the grammar book. We are not meant to draw consequences from it but simply to act in accord with what it sets out.

If by saying that modern linguistics is a descriptive science Lyons means that it only describes, imposing taxonomies just for ease of classification and recognition by us, then that, too, is not a theory any more than a classification system in biology is a theory. It may depend on a theory for why we set up the way we classify, but we are not meant to reason from its classifications to conclusions. The assumption that there are animals and bacteria or that there are mammals and marsupials are no more foundational than saying that there are subjects and predicates in English. They are crucial to that way of classifying but do not make those "sciences" into theories. And it is theories, attempts not only to codify but to explain and predict, that we are concerned with here.[3]

Truth and the construction of models
We reason with prescriptive claims as well as claims that invoke a division between what is right/wrong or correct/incorrect by taking those divisions to be true/false divisions, classifying claims into true ones and false ones. In "Truth and Reasoning" in this volume I set out a justification for doing so, and in "Reasoning with Prescriptive Claims" in this volume you can see that method applied. Only by making the assumption that these divisions of claims into good/bad, just/unjust, correct/incorrect are or can be understood as a division between what is true and what is false are we justified in using our usual methods of reasoning with such claims. And with our usual methods of reasoning come also our usual methods of constructing and evaluating theories.

To say that there are quite distinct methods of constructing and evaluating theories that contain prescriptive or overtly judgmental claims, methods that do not apply to scientific theories, is to take a stand against calling the claims of such theories true or false. In that case, we have to devise and justify what methods of reasoning we shall use with them, for there would be no reason to think that any of the usual methods we employ in physics and chemistry and in our ordinary lives apply. That is a big project, and only on the basis of such an assumption and analysis of how to reason well could someone claim that how we construct and evaluate such theories is—or should be—different from how we construct and evaluate scientific ones. Until someone does that, we have no clear justification for assuming that there is or should be a difference in how we construct and evaluate different kinds of theories.

Let's review, then, how to construct and evaluate a theory, which I presented with examples in "Models and Theories" in *Reasoning in Science and Mathematics*. Then we can consider other ways people propose to evaluate theories.

Constructing and evaluating theories

The data

We are trying to construct a theory that accounts for the data and allows us to make predictions. The data and the predictions are claims, ones we believe are true (or correct, or just, or . . .) and ones we believe are false (or incorrect, or unjust, or . . .).

These may be as simple as "This is a rock," which we feel is indubitable, theory-free.

Or they may be as complex as "There is something moving on the slide under the microscope." A psychologist beginning work in biology may well question why that claim about the reality of what she sees through a microscope is taken as experience, or at least as an obvious deduction from experience. But after the general form of the inference is made explicit once or twice—from direct claims about personal experience to that kind of claim—the psychologist is likely to accept such claims as undisputed evidence. If she doesn't accept them, then she's questioning the basis of that science. Within any one science there is usually a high level of agreement on what counts as an "observational" claim. When new techniques are introduced into a science or when a new area of science is developing, there is often controversy about what counts as experience. Galileo's report of moons around Jupiter was received with considerable skepticism because telescopes were not assumed to be accurate, and indeed at that time they distorted a lot. In ethology, the study of animal behavior in natural settings, there is no agreement yet on what counts as a report on experience, and you can find different journal articles using different standards.[4]

Or the data may consist of claims that seem to be value-laden such as "Torturing dogs is wrong," assuming a whole background on which we do not seem to agree. It is that background, whether in physics, or biology, or ethics, or logic that we wish to draw forward, to make explicit, to be an agreed-upon source from which we can draw conclusions, from which we can justify our classification of claims, from which we can predict and explain.

A path of abstraction
We try to find common themes in the data. We look for why we accept or reject certain examples. We develop some general principles. Those principles are developed along with our setting out what we consider significant in the examples, what we shall pay attention to, for we know that we can't pay attention to all. We abstract from the examples both in what we pay attention to and in what principles we use to make those choices or which are affected by those choices. The adoption of general assumptions about the nature of the world and how we will abstract from our experience are the *path of abstraction* of the theory.[5]

The general principles are not claims of our theories. They are not logical rules such as *modus ponens*, nor moral principles such as the means do not justify the ends, nor physical assumptions such as Newton's laws of motion. All those may be part of our theory. But they are not why we adopt our theory. What we are looking for is why we should accept assumptions such as those. On what basis do we build our theory?

In "Models and Theories" I have given examples of how we abstract and draw general principles in building scientific theories. Let's look here at theories that seem further from science.

For a logical theory, we might say that there is so much in the examples—the claims—that we could pay attention to that we will restrict our focus to only the linguistic structure of certain kinds of sentences in terms of a few sentence connectives like "or" and "if . . . then . . .". We can then restrict our attention further by saying that for the simplest claims, those which are not compounded with these connectives, the only aspect of them we'll consider is whether they are true or false. With some additional assumptions we can then develop classical propositional logic, as I do in *Propositional Logics*. There I also show how different assumptions and choices of what to pay attention to lead to different propositional logics.

In establishing predicate logic, we assume that the world is made up of things. This is no abstraction from experience but an assumption that determines what counts as experience. In accord with it, we restrict our attention to the structure of sentences in terms of the words that refer to specific things—names and pronouns—and what's left over in the sentence when those are extracted which we call predicates. Paying attention to such structure is an abstraction from our experience of talking and reasoning, which is the method I use in *Predicate Logic*.

Classical predicate logic contradicts classical propositional logic. It classifies as true:

> If all men are mortal, and Socrates is a man, then Socrates is mortal.

Classical propositional logic says this need not be true. We maintain, though, that the contradiction is only apparent: we are paying attention to more in classical predicate logic than in classical propositional logic.

In modeling moral judgments, we may say that what we will pay attention to in our experience is whether a sentence offers good advice, treating a sentence that does as true and one that doesn't as false. Then with certain assumptions about how the role of human capabilities are taken into account in deciding what is good advice or bad advice, we can develop a theory of reasoning with prescriptive claims, treating that division as a true/false dichotomy, as I do in "Reasoning with Prescriptive Claims" in this volume.[6]

Theories, whether in science, or ethics, or logic, are best understood as abstractions. The choice of what we pay attention to and what general principles we use can only be true in the sense of correctly representing that part of the world they are meant to represent in a particular situation. We can say of a theory such as Euclidean plane geometry, or the kinetic theory of gases, or classical propositional logic only that it is applicable or not in a particular situation we are investigating, where a "situation" is just some part of what we deem to be experience that we describe using claims.

To say that a theory is applicable is to say that though there are differences between the world and what the assumptions of the theory state, those differences don't matter for the conclusions we wish to draw. Often we can decide if a theory is applicable only by attempting to apply it. We use the theory to draw conclusions in particular situations, claiming that the differences don't matter. If the conclusions—the predictions—turn out to be true (enough), then we have some confidence that we are right. If a prediction turns out to be false, then the model is not applicable there.

The question is not whether the axioms of a theory are true, even if those who created it intended that. The question is under what circumstances we can use the theory. In what situations do the similarities that are being invoked hold and the differences not matter? There will always be much in a situation that is not taken into account in a theory, for we do not and cannot pay attention to all. The question is whether what isn't taken into account matters for our having confidence in the conclusions we draw from the theory in this situation. Thus, Newton's laws of motion are useful in designing automobiles since the assumptions that the world is made up of things and that we will not pay attention to the quantum nature of the materials involved leads us to true (enough) conclusions. Thus, classical propositional logic is useful when we are concerned only with the truth or falsity of our simplest claims, though in other situations we may wish to take account of subject matter or how we might come to know whether such claims are true or false.

When we make predictions and they are true, we confirm a range of application of a model. When we make predictions and they are false, we establish limits for the range of application of the model. More information about where the model can be applied and where it cannot may lead, often with great effort, to our describing more precisely the range of application of a model. In that case, the claims describing the range of application can be added to the theory.

Eventually we hope to find theories whose range of application can be precisely and clearly stated, where we can say that the theory is applicable whenever this is the case, where we are justified in saying that the axioms of the theory are true.

How then do we judge a theory?

Evaluating theories
We derive consequences from our prescriptive theories, and true (enough) ones help to establish a range of application of the theory. But what about false or anomalous consequences?

Newton's laws of motion do not correctly predict the paths of rays of light from distant stars when the light passes close to the sun. Classical propositional logic classifies as true "If the moon is made of green cheese, then $2 + 2 = 4$," which seems at best anomalous. An ethical theory that endorses the Golden Rule justifies the actions of a sadist who is also a masochist.

When we encounter such consequences of a theory, we have the following options (as argued for in "Models and Theories"):

(1) If we have constructed the theory with a clear path of abstraction, then tracing back along that path we can try to distinguish what difference there is between our model and our experience that matters. What have we ignored in this situation that cannot be ignored?

(a) If we can see such a difference and state it in some general way, we can modify the theory to take account of that further aspect.

(b) If we cannot state precisely what difference it is that matters, then at best the false prediction sets some limit on the range of application of the model or theory. We cannot use the theory here—where "here" means this situation or ones that we can see are very similar.

(c) If, however, we find that such consequences are too numerous, too difficult to accommodate with further restrictions, or if there is another theory that does not yield those contradictions yet which we can use to deduce the key claims that the original theory was meant to explain, then we abandon the theory.

Still, there are cases when we retain the theory even though it clearly contradicts experience. Astronomers tell us that the earth revolves around the sun, yet we see the sun travel across the sky while we are standing still. Physicists tell us that a table is mostly empty space, yet we knock on it and know it is solid. We accept the theory despite these apparent contradictions because:

(2) We draw further consequences from the theory and use those along with observations about our perceptual capabilities to explain why such anomalous claims are not in contradiction with the theory.

True predictions are never enough to justify a theory. Indeed, the problem is that we do not "justify" a theory nor show that it is "valid." What we do in the process of testing predictions is show how and where the theory can be applied. And for us to have confidence in that, either we must show that the claims in the theory are true or show in what situations the differences between what is represented and the abstraction of it in the theory do not matter. True (enough) predictions can help in that. But equally crucial is our ability to trace the path of abstraction so that we can see what has been ignored in our modeling and why true predictions serve to justify our ignoring those aspects of experience. Without that clear path of abstraction, all we can do is try to prove that the claims in the theory are actually true. Without that clear path or without reason to believe the claims are true, we have no reason to trust the predictions of a theory.

To summarize:

- We create theories by abstracting from our experience.
- True predictions from such a theory confirm a range of application of the theory.
- False consequences from such a theory can be accommodated by either:
  - Modifying the theory to account for more of our experience.
  - Restricting the range of application of the theory.
  - Explaining the anomaly in terms of human perceptual capabilities.
- False predictions that cannot be accommodated in those ways lead us to abandon the theory. Either the resulting range of application is too small, or another theory works better for a wider range of application, or we see that we have assumed something in addition to our experience that the false predictions lead us to believe is false.

Consistency

In evaluating a theory, we excise or explain away contradictions. Or if the contradictions between what the theory predicts and the claims we accept are too fundamental or numerous, we abandon the theory. We do so because we believe that a theory and our judgments of the data should be consistent.

Consistency is an imperative of rationality. We adopt it for what we deem to be "objective" data in the sciences because we believe there is a world external to us (parts of) which our theory is meant to describe. That world is coherent, out there, and if we use language correctly no two contradictory claims can both be true. Absolutely fundamental not only in our theory building but in our notion of rationality and in every part of our daily life is the assumption that a sentence cannot be both true and false, that the false is the opposite of the true.

But why should we accept the imperative of consistency for divisions of propositions into correct/incorrect, just/unjust, or any of the other divisions on which we base theories? That is a big question that I deal with in "Truth and Reasoning" in this volume. Briefly, in practice we do require consistency, and we do so because without it we have no guide for how to reason.[7] If we say that such divisions are inherently prescriptive, we have an additional motive to adopt consistency: we do not want to conclude that we should both do and not do. A moral dilemma that we have good reason to classify as both true and false is as unwelcome as the liar paradox, and in both cases we reject such sentences as claims, as I discuss in "Truth and Reasoning."

Perhaps we do not have the same confidence in our data for theories based on such divisions as we do for the data of physics or biology. Some of our judgments of what is good reasoning and what is bad, or of what are ethical actions and what are unethical are clearly contradictory or else can easily be shown to lead to contradictions. But really, we should say that they can more easily be shown to lead to contradictions. It is a matter of degree, not kind, that our data, our judgments of experience, may be contradictory. Without some explanation of the inherent difference between such divisions and the "objective" division of the true and false, and, based on that, a clear analysis of how to reason with such divisions, we have no reason to abandon the imperative of rationality that our theories and judgments should be consistent.

The path of abstraction is crucial
Crucial to our evaluation of theories is our ability to trace the path of abstraction so that we can see what has been ignored in our modeling and why the true/good/correct predictions serve to justify our ignoring those aspects of experience. Without that clear path of abstraction and a clear statement of the fundamental assumptions we make in constructing a theory, we have no guide for whether to accept the theory or abandon it in the face of contradictions with our less fundamental or unanalyzed intuitions.

But some disagree.

Axiomatic constructions of theories

Some people construct theories syntactically. They set out axioms and say that those define the theory. They wish to avoid metaphysical assumptions, eschewing a path of abstraction, in favor of what they say is the greater clarity of inspecting axioms. Different people may have quite different assumptions about why to adopt the axioms yet still agree that the axioms are correct. That we need not agree on those assumptions is a virtue of this approach, they say.

Relevance logics, for example, have been constructed in this way. What should we do, then, when one person says that "If dogs bark and dogs chase cats, then dogs chase cats" is a failure of relevance, yet it's a consequence of the system?

Moral theories have been constructed in this way. What should we do, then, when by assuming the Golden Rule we justify that the sadist is good when she tortures since she is also a masochist who likes to be tortured?

If we have arrived at the theory by a process of abstraction from examples, saying that this is what we consider important in them and that not, then we can go back along that path of abstraction and see if there is something in the examples that we have deemed unimportant which in this new case—where the prediction is wrong—is important. Thus, though classical propositional logic can be presented entirely syntactically, when we have doubts about its applicability we return to a path of abstraction, whether that be in terms of modeling the properties and relations of abstract propositions or in terms of modeling our ordinary speech and reasoning. There need not be a single path of abstraction to arrive at a theory, and in dealing with contradictions or anomalies in the theory we may have recourse to one or the other of those. Different paths may lead to different resolutions of the contradictions or anomalies.

But if the principles are stated as axioms without a semantic and metaphysical basis, we have to begin to examine our metaphysical assumptions so we can fill in that path of abstraction. Or, fleeing metaphysics, we tinker with the theory, modifying the axiomatic principles so that they apply here but don't apply there, saying that this syntactic principle takes precedence over that example. But then, as relevance logicians and ethical theorists who give theories (almost) entirely syntactically find, we have no clear way to evaluate a theory. We can judge a theory only by its consequences, they say. True consequences confirm the theory; false ones disconfirm it.

But if to confirm a theory means that it is now clear that it can be applied in these kinds of situations, then that's the process of evaluating theories discussed previously. We try to set out more clearly what exactly the situations are, and to do that we need a path of abstraction.

If to confirm a theory by means of its consequences means to prove that its axioms are true, or at least more probably true, then that is the method of inference to the best explanation, which is fallacious reasoning.[8] Worse, it isn't even clear that we ever have good reason to say that the axioms of a theory are true rather than that they set out the conditions in which we are justified in using the theory.

But some say there is a particular way to invoke consequences of a theory in order to justify the theory that does not involve a path of abstraction, which what we'll look at next.

The method of reflective equilibrium

Some say we can and should judge a theory solely by its consequences using the *method of reflective equilibrium*. Rosanna Keefe in her book *Theories of Vagueness* gives the clearest and fullest presentation of that view I have seen.[9] In the second appendix here, I examine the way she uses that method to justify her own theory of vagueness as a case study of the application of the ideas discussed in this section.

Here is how Keefe describes the method:

> Theorists should aim to find the best balance between preserving as many as possible of our judgments or opinions of various different kinds (some intuitive and pre-philosophical, others more theoretical) and meeting such requirements on theories as simplicity. And when counter-intuitive consequences do follow, the theorist needs to be able to explain *why* we are inclined to make those judgments that their theory regards as erroneous. . . .
>
> It is a holistic method: we assess a theory as a whole, by its overall success, allowing counter-intuitive consequences in one part of the theory for the sake of saved intuitions in another part. I do not assume that the best is good enough: it may be that no extant theory of the relevant phenomenon preserves enough intuitions to be acceptable, though I shall not now enter into the difficult question of how good is good enough. p. 38 [underlining added]

> Theorists should be most reluctant to deny very widely held judgements or those held among the experts thought most appropriate to judge the matter in question. . . . And they should have a similar regard for those most deeply held, i.e. that we are least prepared to revise. There will also be intuitions and judgements that are particularly important in the context, namely when giving a theory of vagueness. Certain opinions

which could be ignored in another context are crucial because to ignore them would be to ignore a key factor bound up with vagueness. . . .

Given the described methodology, there is unlikely to be any theory which can be conclusively defended: the strategy invites different equilibria reached by choosing to retain different judgements and justifying the sacrifices by emphasising different gains. And apart from showing a theory to be inconsistent, there will be no test which will refute a theory by showing its incompatibility with certain apparent truths—any apparent truth on which such a test would need to rest may be denied if this is compensated for by those retained and by other virtues the theory can boast. In assessing some given theory, we should determine the extent and range of judgements which it is forced to deny to reach its equilibrium. Controversy over the success of different theories can then arise in at least three different ways.

First, there can be disputes about what is the relevant body of opinions—whether some given opinion is really one that we must attempt to save. It may take a (carefully formulated) questionnaire to discover what the opinion of folks really are. (And it must not be assumed that the corrupted views of the theorising philosopher reflect the common view.) Then, in some cases, two theorists can agree that there is some relevant judgement that we should try to preserve, but disagree over what its content is. One theorist's presentation of an intuitive judgement can be seen by another as prejudiced by the theory advocated. . . . [presents an example]

Second, even if there were agreement over what judgements should be preserved, there could be disagreement concerning some particular theory over which of those judgements it does and does not preserve. Determining the counter-intuitive consequences of a theory is always a major part of its assessment. And we must be cautious of theories that appear to save the, or some of the, high-profile intuitions (e.g. regarding the law of excluded middle) but that do so in a way that requires the denial of a range of other lower profile, but equally important, intuitions.

Third, if we are to have some theories in front of us, along with a list of their counter-intuitive consequences, there could still be considerable disagreement over which of those theories provides the best fit for our body of opinions and intuitions. For it needs to be settled what costs are incurred by denying particular judgements and what would count as adequate compensation for denying them. Different parties to the debate will inevitably value different opinions differently and the methodology does not solve these disagreements.
pp. 40–41

The method of reflective equilibrium is primarily a method of evaluating theories. It can, to a minimal extent, also figure in the methodology of constructing theories of vagueness . . . . But reflective equilibrium does allow theorists to come up with their theory however they like. (Though the merits of a methodology of construction can only be judged by the success according to the reflective equilibrium criteria of the resulting theories.)

There is, I suggest, no possible alternate methodology. Theorists may not be open about their search for a reflective equilibrium of the kind described, but this merely results in them privileging certain intuitions, opinions or considerations and ignoring others; it does not reveal that they have a better methodology to hand or any way of justifying their selection of the constraints that cannot be violated. The methodology I describe recommends assessing a theory on all the evidence available. All we have to go on, apart from equally inconclusive theoretical considerations already factored in, is linguistic practice in the form of what we (speakers) say and believe and how we reason. My described methodology cannot ensure that theorists take account of all relevant information, but stressing the absence of a unique, small set of over-riding constraints could encourage better practice. p.42

Finally, discussing her particular model of how to reason with vagueness, she says:

We do not need a prior justification of the use of the apparatus independent of the account it delivers. p. 42

It seems that Keefe means her method to apply to "judgmental" theories only, not scientific ones. But all her comments apply equally to scientific theories. If her method is not meant to be applicable to theories in physics, biology, ecology, and chemistry, then she owes us an explanation about how theories in logic and ethics are so different from those. And that, we have seen, is difficult if not impossible without assuming that those "judgmental" theories involve a notion of truth that is quite different from "objective" truth in scientific theories, in which case she owes us an explanation why we should adopt any of our usual methods of reasoning in developing such theories and deriving consequences from them. Since she doesn't do that, let's assume that her methodology is meant for the evaluation of any theory. Though we don't have to decide whether it is better for a chemical theory to preserve the judgment that water freezes rather than that lead does not float, we might have to judge whether it is better for it to predict the heat of a gas or to describe certain quantum effects.

The method of reflective equilibrium says that we have to judge a theory by its consequences. That is the entire thrust of Keefe's view, as is evident in the underlined part and the last quotation. The intuitions and judgments she says we must weigh are those that are or could be consequences of our theory; they are not judgments and intuitions that stand behind the theory as a whole, such as, for predicate logic and Newtonian physics, that the world is made up of things. That's clear, in part, because she allows that theorists can make up their theories any way they like, which includes the axiomatic method. And in applying the method in her own work on vagueness she does not weigh any fundamental assumptions about the nature of the world, as you can see in Appendix 2 here.

In using this method, how are we to decide which judgments (intuitions) to accept and which to reject?

It is disingenuous to suggest that we might use a questionnaire to discover what ordinary folks think in devising a physical theory, or a biological theory, or an ethical theory, or a logical theory. The one study I know that does attempt it for logic shows just how wrong philosophers have been in saying that their assumptions reflect ordinary views.[10]

To give priority to widely held authorities is a conservative injunction that would have led to the rejection of the ideas of Boole, De Morgan, and Frege in logic, to the rejection of the theories of the epicureans or G.E. Moore in ethics, and to the rejection of the work of Galileo in astronomy. In any case, there is often greater dispute about who should be considered the generally accepted authorities than there is about the particular judgments under consideration. And if someone is deemed such an authority, soon enough serious criticism is put forward to try to refute his or her judgments.

Nor is it a clear standard to say that we should give precedence to judgments that we are least prepared to revise. That would seem to be based on only a reluctance to revise our opinions—if we knew who the "we" are.

Keefe says that there is no alternate methodology. But there is: create a clear path of abstraction to the model. The judgments and intuitions that are used are clearly ordered in priority. The grand assumptions that generate the theory as a whole, clarified by the method of abstraction, are what we have to accept or reject relative to consequences of the theory that might contradict particular judgments that we find acceptable/true. We not only have a clear scale of weighing judgments, we have a way to modify the theory beyond tinkering with what amounts to a syntactic presentation of the theory without any semantic underpinning.

Without basing our work on clearly enunciated fundamental principles that we use to choose our axioms, we have no guide to whether we should accept or reject a theory.

Conclusion

There seems to be no principled way to distinguish between what are often called descriptive theories and prescriptive theories. Both involve judgments, and the data of both are open to revision. Only if we could distinguish the methods of classification of claims of prescriptive theories from the classification of claims as true or false and set out what methods of reasoning are acceptable with such divisions, could we have a basis for claiming that the method of construction and evaluation of prescriptive theories is or should be different from that of descriptive theories.

We construct theories by a process of abstraction based on some general metaphysical principles and choices of what we shall pay attention to. Doing so allows us to judge theories by seeing how false or anomalous consequences of the theory can be accommodated by modifying the path of abstraction or invoking some human capabilities as constraints on the evaluation of the claims. When such false or anomalous consequences cannot be accommodated, we have good reason to either abandon the theory or settle for quite restricted applications of it. Judging a theory solely by its consequences mistakes the nature of theories and yields no way to evaluate or modify a theory in the face of false or anomalous consequences of it.

Appendix 1 Evaluating ethical theories

Two scholars have investigated in a particularly clear way problems in evaluating ethical theories. Commenting on those will illuminate the discussions in this essay.

Jonathan Dancy in "Moral Epistemology" says:

> A *particularist* epistemology takes it that our first awareness is of facts which are restricted to the particular case before us; we may hope to move on from these later and come to grasp more general truths, but we have to start with the particular case. Philosophies of science are commonly particularist in this sense, for good reason. A *generalist* epistemology holds that we first become aware of general truths which we are then able to apply to particular cases as they come along. This approach is unconvincing in most areas, but it has gained many adherents in moral epistemology. Many theorists find themselves holding that we learn moral principles first, and that there is nothing in a particular case that one could extract a principle from; one has to learn it in other ways, directly.   p. 287

The particularist view is what I have described in terms of abstracting. The generalist epistemology is compatible more with the view of those who hold that there is a basis for our theories that is entirely objective and which we might have insight into without experience.

Dancy continues:

> I turn now to particularist approaches to moral epistemology. I start with the views of W. D. Ross. Ross held that what we learn first is a feature that makes a difference to how we should act *here*. ... Given this entirely particular knowledge, however, we can immediately move to something general. For we recognize by a process called *intuitive induction* that what makes a difference here must make the same difference wherever it occurs. So we can learn the truth of a moral principle from what we can see in the particular case; the principle is self-evident to us, since nothing more is necessary to reveal it than what the present case contains.
>
> Intuitive induction is perhaps an unfamiliar process. Its use is not however confined to ethics. An example Ross gives is that of discovering the truth of a principle of inference (*modus ponens*, say) by seeing it in the soundness of one instance. The soundness of the inference "If he is here he'll kill her: he is here: so he will kill her" is one which reveals to those that can see it the soundness of the principle "If p then q: p: so q".   p. 288

But the problem remains. How can we see the truth of a principle from just one instance? We never have just one instance from which we see a fundamental principle. Rather, we have a pattern of such instances that we have amassed over our lifetime, and when we look at a particular instance, wondering for the first time why it is right, we can sometimes, though very rarely, articulate a general principle such as *modus ponens*. In my experience it is rare for anyone to clearly articulate a general principle that governs even one such instance, a general principle that would guarantee the correctness/aptness/truth of the instance. Ask anyone why it's correct to infer from "If you won't wash the dishes, I won't take you to the movies" and "You didn't wash the dishes" to "I won't take you to the movies." Most can't even see this as an instance of *modus ponens*. And those who can, who have thought about the forms of claims, are almost invariably inarticulate about why that principle is correct. It's just correct, they say. It's only a few who have thought more deeply about the subject who say that the principle follows from some general assumptions about reasoning and truth, seeing it as one instance of a more general pattern that includes other instances. And they, and I, are nearly inarticulate about why such deeper principles are correct/apt/true. We can say only: that's the fundamental metaphysics we adopt. There is no ultimate justification of a metaphysics through reasoning. It might seem that this is Ludwig Wittgenstein's view, as described by Dancy:

> A different approach to the nature of moral justification would be to use the ideas of Wittgenstein [*On Certainty*]. We could see certain moral beliefs as "frame" beliefs which play in ethics the role played in ordinary perceptual justification by such beliefs as "I have two hands" and "The sun is a very long way away". These "frame" beliefs are not justified but stand in no need of justification; they are the things we appeal to in the justification of other beliefs. Candidates would be "All have equal rights" and "One should not torture innocent children". This would give us something of the structure of foundationalism but from a completely different perspective.   p. 290

But this is to take certain judgments as axiomatic, not developing a semantic underpinning for our ethical judgments.

Jeff McMahan in "Moral Intuition" gives far greater weight to intuition than to theory:

> It is instructive to consider how most of us respond when, on inquiring into a particular moral problem, we find that a moral theory has implications for the problem that clash with our intuitions. Our response is not to question how well grounded the theory is, on the assumption that we should be prepared to acquiesce if we find that the theory is well supported. If the theory generates its conclusion

via a distinct argument, our tendency is to detach the argument from the parent theory and consider it on its own merits. According to R. M. Hare, for example, his universal prescriptivist theory of morality implies that we should reason about the morality of abortion by applying a variant of the Golden Rule: "we should do to others as we are glad that they did do to us". When we discover that this principle implies (according to Hare) not only that abortion is wrong (if other things are equal) but also that remaining childless is wrong (again if other things are equal), we do not go back to Hare's earlier books to check the arguments for universal prescriptivism. Instead we undertake an independent inquiry to try to determine whether and, if so, to what extent it matters to the morality of abortion that, when an abortion is not performed, there will typically be a person who is glad to exist who would not have existed if the abortion had been performed. That is, if we are serious about understanding the morality of abortion, we will take seriously the considerations identified as relevant by the theory; and we may be grateful to the theory for helping us to see whatever relevance these considerations may in fact have; but we are generally not overawed by the fact that these considerations have been identified as relevant *by the theory*. Their provenance in the theory fails to impress. p. 98

Examples matter. But the theory does, too, and it is prescriptive rationally: if you believe this and this, if you accept such and so assumptions, then you should accept the consequences of those assumptions. In particular, in such and so case you can see that if you hold to those assumptions you'll get a consequence that seems odd or wrong. Well, either you need to modify what you think of as odd or wrong because you hold those assumptions to be determinate, or else you need to find some way to modify the theory by adding further assumptions that differentiate the situation under consideration from others that the previous assumptions classed as the same, or you say that the theory was too far wrong in its consequences and abandon it.

As for McMahan's example, I certainly would go back to Hare's theory and try to find out how he got such an anomalous result. But I would be willing to modify my view that the result is anomalous if I were to find that his arguments for universal prescriptivism along those lines are convincing.

It is not that moral intuition is not important or relevant any more than logical intuition is not relevant to studies of logic. It is that we owe it to ourselves to go as deeply as we can in uncovering our implicit assumptions that govern our evaluation of particular examples. And once we uncover those assumptions, we need to consider whether they are in fact what we do or should accept. One way is by testing them against further examples. In doing so we modify and clarify them, eventually building what McMahan wants to consider only perjoratively: a theory. But a theory is just a codification of what we have discovered about how to proceed in our reasoning in a subject. I won't disagree with McMahan that many theories are inadequately grounded in our intuitions and hence that we need concern ourselves not so much with the theory as the particular argument. But I do not draw the conclusion, as McMahan does, that therefore moral theories are just stimuli to our own intuitions.

McMahan discusses other views, too.

> Coherentist accounts of moral justification hold that a moral belief is justified solely in terms of its relations, particularly its inferential relations, with other beliefs. It is justified to the extent that it coheres well with a set of beliefs that together form a coherent whole. By contrast, foundationalist accounts hold that some beliefs are self-justifying—at least in the sense that they are justified independently of their relation to other beliefs. According to foundationalist accounts, a moral belief is justified if and only if it is either self-justifying or bears an appropriate inferential relation to a belief that is self-justifying. p. 100

The coherentist view of moral justification is incoherent for the same reason that the coherence theory of truth is incoherent. The latter says, roughly, that we should abandon the usual notion of truth as correspondence or relative to some standard. Claims are true or false as they cohere with other claims in our general understanding of the world. Coherence is invariably explained to require at least consistency: one claim A does not cohere with others if together they are not consistent. But then we have to ask what notion of consistency is intended. For simple claims this might not be a problem.

But for complex ones some method of reasoning, some logic must be invoked, whether that be implicit and informal or fully formalized. Then we must ask why we should adopt that logic as our standard. Every logic is either explicitly or implicitly based on some semantic analysis of propositions. Such assumptions are needed to give a justification of both the propositions taken as axiomatic in the logic and the methods of inference allowed. But we cannot invoke coherence for justifying the logic because we need the logic to define coherence. The coherence theory of truth is an attempt to substitute a syntactical analysis in place of a semantic analysis, with no justification for the syntactical analysis. Similarly, the coherentist view of moral justification gives no guidance for what claims we take as fundamental, nor what logic we should adopt in reasoning about moral judgments, while assuming, without justification, that consistency in reasoning is the most fundamental of all judgments. It is a serious question what logical principles should be employed in reasoning about moral judgments, as you can see in the essay "Reasoning with Prescriptive Claims" in this volume.

McMahan then discusses the status of intuitions:

It seems implausible to regard our intuitions themselves as foundational. This seems to attribute to them too exalted a status. While our
intuitions do seem to have a certain initial credibility, it seems exor-
bitant to suppose that they are self-evident or self-justifying. We
recoil from the suggestion (advanced, as I noted earlier, by various
traditional Intuitionists) that intuitions are the unshakable basis on
which all moral knowledge rests.

There are, however, at least two ways of overcoming this ground
of reluctance to combine foundationalism with the Intuitive Approach.
The first is to recognize that a belief may be of the foundational *sort*
and yet be defeasible. Suppose, for example, that sense perceptions
are the foundations of empirical knowledge. Even if all empirical
knowledge is derived immediately from sense perceptions, it does not
follow that *all* sense perceptions are sources of empirical knowledge.
Some may be distorted, illusory, or otherwise erroneous. And there is
no reason why the same may not be true, *mutatis mutandis*, in the
case of moral intuitions. It is, of course, paradoxical to claim that a
belief that is self-justifying may actually be unjustified or mistaken.
But the idea that a belief is self-justifying is not meant to entail that the
belief is necessarily justified. To say that a belief is self-justifying is
to say only that, insofar as the belief is in fact justified, it is not
justified by virtue of its inferential relations with other beliefs. p. 101

But then we have the problem of how we distinguish between good/true/
reliable intuitions and bad/false/unreliable ones. Either it is because of some
further intuition, or . . . what? If you say we do it via constraints on generality
and consistency, that is putting the intuition that we ought to have generality
and consistency at the foundation, and how do we know that that intuition isn't
bad/false/unreliable? Some intuitions simply have to be admitted; we can only
point, show, lead by example, help to obtain an insight to convince someone of
their rightness. That is what the mystics, the religious, the people of any "way"
do, whether Catholic, Zen, or pyrrhonian skeptic.

The role of general principles is what McMahan discusses next.

But there is a deeper basis for trying to subsume an intuition under a
principle that is itself supported by its power to unify and explain a
range of intuitions. This is that the process of achieving increasing
coherence among principles and intuitions facilitates the discovery of
one's deeper values and also brings one's surface beliefs about particular cases into alignment with those deeper values in a way that
reveals and illuminates the connections between them. When one
seeks to formulate a moral principle that implies and illuminates
one's intuition about a particular problem or case, one is in fact

groping or probing for one's own deeper values. The expectation that the principle will illuminate and explain the force of the intuition assumes that the intuition is in fact an expression or manifestation, in a particular context, of a moral belief that is deeper, more basic, and more general than the intuition itself. One's efforts to formulate the principle and to revise and refine it in a way that brings more and more of one's intuitions within its scope are attempts to capture or articulate some core moral belief in its full generality, to get its form exactly right, omitting nothing, however subtle.   pp. 103–104

This is closer to the methodology I present; it holds equally for any model. But for modeling in ethics there may be no core belief already there. It may be that we have a heterogeneous collection of particular intuitions that we try to amalgamate by searching for a general principle, and the general principle may not be one that we would have previously adopted but adopt now only because it seems right as it unifies a lot—though rarely all—of our particular intuitions. Again, it seems that our intuition that our reasoning must be consistent takes precedence over any other intuition we have.

Appendix 2   Rosanna Keefe's analysis of vagueness

In this appendix I examine Rosanna Keefe's use of the method of reflective equilibrium in the construction and evaluation of her theory of vagueness that she presents in *Theories of Vagueness*. I am not attempting to give a deep analysis of vagueness in reasoning here, for, as I explain in "Truth and Reasoning" in this volume, I think that no such deep analysis is needed.

Vague predicates
Keefe takes vagueness to be an aspect of predicates such as "is bald" or "is smarter than." Apparently, this is the common view today.

This assumption rules out viewing her theory as descriptive of abstract things such as propositions, facts, or thoughts. The usual conception of abstract predicates does not allow for a predicate to be vague, and she presents no other view of abstract predicates, nor does she talk about vague or bad applications of abstract predicates. So the predicates of which she speaks must be linguistic units. And the judgments she discusses are about what we accept or do not accept about how to reason well. Keefe, however, doesn't present any sociological or psychological studies.

To talk of predicates is to construe the world as made up at least in part of things and to restrict our attention to assertions that we can construe as being about things. That is a major metaphysical assumption. It's not necessarily suspect, for, after all, it's the basis of much of our ordinary speech. But it excludes consideration of vagueness in reasoning about masses or about the world as process.[11] Nor does Keefe consider the view that vagueness is an aspect of sentences as wholes and not of parts of sentences, which can accommodate a wider scope of metaphysics.[12]

Even within the tradition of reasoning about the world as made up of things and within the view that it is parts of speech that are vague, the restriction to considering vagueness only of predicates eliminates any analysis of quantifying words such as "most" or "many" that apparently contribute to vagueness.

These observations need not be a criticism of Keefe's approach. She takes it as given that we have a clear method of how to reason with predicates that are not vague: classical predicate logic. Her goal is to show how to extend or modify that method to incorporate reasoning with vague predicates. So it is within that tradition we should evaluate her work.

Making a vague predicate precise

Keefe's method of dealing with vague predicates is based on a way we sometimes deal with vagueness. For example, there may be a question about whether a plant is a bush or a tree. When confronted with this, a botanist may decide to clarify the issue by giving a definition that makes the terms "bush" and "tree" precise, saying that, for example, for a species of plant to be a tree, mature specimens must have a main trunk that is at least 35 cm in diameter with all other branches 25% smaller in diameter. That is, a botanist, or we in some situations, may eliminate vagueness by decree.

We don't do this often, and we know that when we do we're no longer dealing with the same predicate we started with. But when it seems appropriate to do so, converting a word or phrase into a precise predicate solves all problems with how to reason with it, for then we can employ classical predicate logic.

There will always be more than one way to make a vague predicate precise —if there weren't, the predicate wouldn't be vague. Another botanist may disagree with the first and say that for a species of plant to be a tree any mature specimen must have a diameter of at least 47 cm. Another might say that's too much; at least 42 cm is enough, with other branches, however, at least 40% smaller in diameter. To understand how to reason with vague predicates, says Keefe, we have to consider a predicate such as "is a tree" or "is bald" in terms of a range of ways of making it precise, which she calls *precisifications*. She says:

> By taking account of *all* precisifications we can provide the logic
> and semantics of vague language. It is proposed that a sentence is
> true iff it is true on all precisifications, false iff false on all
> precisifications, and neither true nor false otherwise. p. 154

Keefe does not describe her work as seizing on one way that we deal with vagueness and abstracting from that; that is my attempt to make sense of what she is doing. She presents her notion of precisification as a way that might get us a solution to problems of vagueness which is to be judged solely in terms of its consequences.

What counts as an acceptable way to make a predicate precise? No botanist is going to accept a definition of "tree" that says a mature specimen must have a main branch of at least 1/2 cm diameter and all other branches at least 1% less in diameter. Whatever we mean by "tree," it's not that. Keefe says:

> My description of supervaluationism has so far left open the question whether there is a well-defined range of precisifications of e.g. "tall" (a precise set of alternatives between which we are undecided), or whether that range is itself vague, with some candidate precisifications neither clearly counting as precisifications, nor clearly failing to count. This question ties in with the issue of higher-order vagueness, for if there is a precise set of precisifications of "tall", the borderline cases of that predicate will be sharply bounded and the phenomenon of higher-order vagueness must be denied (or, at best, accommodated as a phenomenon of a radically different character to first-order vagueness). If the range of precisifications of "tall" is *not* precise, then the expression "precisification of tall" and the general notion of " precisification" will themselves be vague. Since these are expressions of the metalanguage used to construct the theory, we reach the familiar conclusion that the key elements of the metalanguage must be vague. p. 161–162

Keefe gives no theory of how to reason with the vague predicate "is a good precisification" except to say that to resolve how to reason with vagueness in the metalanguage, we'll have to ascend to a meta-metalanguage, and so on.

> For if vagueness is, in general, to be understood in terms of a multiplicity of precisifications, then accepting the vagueness of "admissible specification" will commit us to a multiplicity of *its* precisifications, which will be modelled in a meta-metalanguage. I argue that such iteration is innocuous. p. 207

To actually reason with this theory, you need to have a stopping place without vagueness. Either that or you adopt a pragmatic approach at some level—for Keefe it's the first meta-level. But then why not adopt a pragmatic approach at the object-language level? Keefe says:

> There is no vicious infinite regress forced upon us. It is just that the vague is not reducible to the non-vague. p. 208

So Keefe's analysis will fail not only to give an analysis of vagueness arising from parts of speech other than predicates, it will deal with only certain predicates, ones suitable to be part of an object language.

Keefe is assuming that there is or needs to be a distinction between language and metalanguage. The usual reason for such a distinction is to avoid the liar paradox according to the now most-accepted solution of that. Absent worries about the liar paradox or other problems of self-reference, there is no obvious motive for distinguishing between some of our speech being part of an object language and some being part of a metalanguage.[13]

Keefe says:

> The theory . . . provides an illuminating and non-trivial account of
> the central features of vagueness, namely borderline cases, the lack
> of sharp boundaries, and the sorites paradox. The vagueness of its
> statement of truth-conditions does not threaten these achievements. p. 206

This is to reiterate her view that a theory must be judged by its consequences, though it is not clear what is meant by saying that a theory is illuminating. Yet it seems on the face of it that the vagueness of the truth-conditions does threaten any "achievements" because it requires us to resolve problems of vagueness in our reasoning by using vagueness in our reasoning. But Keefe argues:

> Such valuations do indeed fail to capture all features of the meanings
> of our predicates—after all, the precisifications are not vague and our
> predicates are. But this constitutes no *objection* to the theory, for the
> claim is that it is the quantification over all precisifications that captures
> the meaning of the natural language predicates; the individual precisifi-
> cations need not. p. 190

There is nothing in what she does that suggests that ranging over all ways to make precise a predicate such as "is bald" captures the meaning of that predicate, neither psychological studies nor appeal to a deeper theory of meaning. At best, she might argue that if her theory is accepted as the best way to deal with certain vague predicates—not with vagueness generally, or even vague predicates generally—then we might in the future come to understand those vague predicates in this manner and agree that the meaning of them is given in this way.

Up to this point Keefe has made several major assumptions in devising her theory: (i) the world is made up of things, and we should parse sentences according to that view; (ii) vagueness in resolving vagueness is acceptable; (iii) there is a need for a language-metalanguage distinction. These are not assumptions of her theory but are assumptions she uses in devising her theory. In using them, even if only implicitly, she is establishing a path of abstraction.

Formalizing how to make a vague predicate precise
Keefe does not present a formal theory and models for that, though she speaks as if it is clear how to do so. My discussion here will be equally informal.

Suppose we wish to use predicate logic to analyze how to reason with some particular discourse that includes some clear predicates as well as some vague ones such as "is bald," "is tall," "is a tree." We take those predicates to realize some of the predicate symbols of the formal language of predicate logic, and perhaps we take as well some names to realize some of the name symbols. To have a model, we assign a truth-value to each atomic predication of a non-vague predicate. Given those evaluations, we then have for this single model, for each way we accept as an "admissible specification" of the vague predicates, a distinct sub-model. Thus, we may stipulate that "Ralph is a dog" is true in the model, while "Tek is tall" is true in some of the specifications and false in others. A model M then consists of many specification models, M_1, M_2, ... There will in general be infinitely many of these. For example, heights that make "is tall" precise can be given with infinitely many rational numbers, even though we cannot actually make all such measurements.

We need that the names and assignments of truth-values for atomic predications that do not involve vague predicates are the same in each of the submodels. In this way, classical predicate logic applies to each semi-formal language, and we are talking about the same things in the same way in each submodels except for the vague predicates. Then ranging over all those ways of making the predicates precise, we finally arrive at truth-values for all formulas. As Keefe says,

> The supervaluation quantifies over these admissible specifications: a sentence is super-true (super-false) iff true (false) on all of them; and truth simpliciter is identified with super-truth. p. 162

It would seem that every atomic predication that involves a vague predicate is neither true nor false in these models. "Tek is tall," "Ralph is bald," "x is a tree" where x refers to the left-most plant in the row of plants outside my office are neither true nor false, for in some of the specifications they will be true and in some false. Similarly, it would seem, every negation of an atomic predication is neither true nor false: " ~ (Tek is tall)," "~ (Ralph is bald)," "~ (x is a tree)" are all neither true nor false. This seems to be casting out all sentences with vague predicates from the realm of those that can be relied on to infer truths. We seem to be in a three-valued logic, with values "true," "false," and "undetermined," where only "true" is designated.

But Keefe rejects that view. There may be some predications with vague predicates that are true (or false) in all models; the example she gives is "Wilt Chamberlain was tall." That's because the range of ways of making a particular predicate precise that we adopt will always make that particular predication true (or always false).

Moreover, even in cases where the range of ways of making a predicate precise does not yield a truth-value for a particular atomic predication, that range can still yield that a compound proposition using that predication is true. An example she gives is to suppose that Tim is shorter than Tek. Then, though "Tim is tall" and "Tek is tall" are both neither true nor false, the following is true:

(a)   If Tim is tall, then Tek is tall.

We can make this analysis clearer by assuming that "is shorter than" is not a vague predicate and is part of the semi-formal language, so that in the model "Tim is shorter than Tek" is true.

But nothing Keefe has presented about models ensures that (a) is true. Even were "is tall" not vague, say we were evaluating (a) in one of the specifications, (a) can come out false, for the predications in it are atomic and hence their evaluations are not linked.

We can force (a) to be true in classical predicate logic, and hence in each specification, in the usual way we ensure that the evaluations of certain atomic predicates are linked in classical predicate logic by assuming an axiom that restricts what models we consider:

$$\forall x \; \forall y \; (\; (x \text{ is shorter than } y) \rightarrow (x \text{ is tall} \rightarrow y \text{ is tall}) \;)$$

Indeed, this is the only way we can deal with such connections in classical predicate logic.[14]

But Keefe does not do that. She ensures that such sentences come out true by restricting the ways we can make predicates precise in what, so far as I can see, is a completely informal manner. That range, though, could be specified at least in part by assuming axioms like this one. Why not specify the range of acceptable ways to make predicates precise entirely using axioms? To do that would be to eliminate the vagueness of the predicate "is an acceptable way to make predicates precise," which she won't allow.

Preserving classical predicate logic

All the classical tautologies, even those which involve vague predicates, are true in each supervaluation model. This is not because of how we restrict the ways to make make vague predicates precise. It is because we use a logic of precise predicates, classical predicate logic, in each of the specifications so that each of the classical tautologies is true in each specification and, hence, true in the entire model.

We can follow the steps to this, but what justification do we have for thinking that the classical tautologies are true when vague predicates occur in them? Why not toss those out as neither true nor false since it is the presence of the vague predicate that is the problem? Keefe wants the classical tautologies to be true so that her work can be seen as an extension of classical logic.

Next take the sentence "either Tek is tall or he is not tall". This is true, since it is true on all precisifications (even if Tek is actually borderline tall when, again, neither disjunct is true). More generally, $p \vee \sim p$ is true whatever the substitution for p and whatever value (or lack of value) p takes: the logical truth of the law of excluded middle is maintained.   pp. 163–164

Keefe presents an ersatz classical logic. We know that "A or not A" is false. It is not the case that either A is true or its negation is true in her semantics. The supervaluationist will say that I've just slipped back into the standard semantics for classical logic. But then "or" and "not" don't mean what we thought they meant. They only mean "relative to your particular way of making these vague predicates precise." That is, "Tek is tall or Tek is not tall" does not mean that "Tek is tall" is true or "Tek is tall" is not true. It means that given any way we might make the sentence precise, "Tek is tall" is true or "Tek is tall" is not true. But then why bother to survey all ways of making the predicates "is tall" precise? Why not just say that before we'll reason with "Tek is tall" as a proposition, we need to be more precise about what we mean by "tall"? The answer is that we can't do that and preserve the vagueness of "tall." On any particular way of making "tall" precise, we'll have some anomalies when we consider other propositions.

Why should we retain classical logic? Surely it must be because for sentences that are not (too) vague it is "right." But no argument for that is offered. The problem is that classical logic, even classical propositional logic, comes with metaphysical assumptions about language, about truth, about inference. Keefe wishes to say that we can divide predicates into those that are vague and those that are not, an assumption that is not at all obvious. Classical logic is just fine for those that are not vague, she seems to think. But why? She hasn't investigated whether the assumptions of classical logic are compatible with her other assumptions about vagueness.

"A or not A" is true no matter how we make the predicates in A precise. But why should that mean that the whole proposition is true? Well, her theory gives that. But why should it being true in all "let's pretend" worlds yield that it's true in the "real" world where there is vagueness? All she can do is point to the "good consequences" of accepting her theory.

> If a theory is to capture the truth of penumbral connections of the
> form '$Fa \vee \sim Ga$', for incompatible F and G, then it will also
> count as true '$Fa \vee \sim Fa$': there is no reasonable way of counting
> one true but not the other. And the unassertibility of the latter in
> contrast with the former is explicable, since, as explained, the former
> can be highly informative by saying something about the properties
> of a, in particular, implying that a does not have those properties

that are incompatible with both *F* and *G* (e.g. that it is blue or green and not red), while '*Fa* v ~ *Fa*' is entirely uninformative (saying that it is red or not-red does nothing to narrow the range of its possible shades). p. 164

So the story is much like what classical logicians give about:

(b)   If the moon is made of green cheese, then 2 + 2 = 4.

We have to accept the anomaly that (b) comes out true in order to get a neat theory. But it doesn't really matter because no one would actually use such a sentence. That kind of defense leaves all the interesting part of reasoning to how to apply classical logic. Yes, classical logic is the right way to reason, so long as you're careful in how you use it, and we won't give you rules for that.

But there are rules, bound up with the nature of the assumptions we make in establishing classical logic. We can give an explanation of why (b) comes out true in a classical propositional logic model but yet seems odd: with (b) we want to pay attention to more in our reasoning than just truth-values and form. We can go back along the path of abstraction that we use to establish classical logic to try to model our unease about accepting (b) as true. There's nothing like that here. It's just looking at trade-offs: we want the one type of sentence to come out true, so we're stuck with having the law of excluded middle true, too. But why not work the other way? We don't want the law of excluded middle to be true, so we shouldn't have that other kind of proposition true, too. We can't go back along a path of abstraction to see how we might modify the theory one way or the other to distinguish between these views. Why should one of these intuitions be favored over the other?

Her analysis of the existential quantifier is even more problematic:

Existential quantification displays behaviour similar to that of disjunction: "something is *F*" can be true though no substitution instance is true. Although there is no *h* for which "people of height *h* are tall while people 0.01 inches shorter are not tall" is true, the existentially quantified sentence formed from it, (H) "there is a height *x* such that people of height *x* are tall while people 0.01 inches shorter are not tall", *is* true, since on each precisification some height or other makes it true. pp. 164–165

We can follow the steps that make her example true despite all instances of it being false, but that doesn't resolve anything. The question is what does the existential quantifier mean if we get a situation like she describes? Well, she could say, it means one thing with precise predicates, and another with vague predicates, and you want it to mean the same for both. No, I just want it to have a univocal meaning that corresponds to something like how we normally use "there is," or "there exists;" and though whether a proposition having a vague predicate in it may affect the interpretation of that, we do not deny the usual understanding of those words completely. "Well, 'black' means 'black' except when we're talking about races, in which case it means 'not white'." That's a whole new use of "black" and not a way to use the word that is compatible with the old uses. Again, Keefe only invokes consequences of theories as a way to judge her work:

> And from the fact (if it is one) that supervaluationism disagrees with our intuitive judgement on certain sentences involving "there is", it does not follow that it misinterprets that expression if (as I claim) it gives the best account more generally of our use of "there is" (including the way we reason using it). p. 182–183

But one thing that her theory does not do is give a good account of our use of "there is." We do not normally reason by thinking about all prescifications, leaving the notion of "an acceptable prescification" imprecise. Her theory is a proposal to do away with how we normally reason and substitute her approach. And the reason for doing that is because, she claims, it solves the paradoxes of vagueness and . . . well, all the rest about trade-offs on what we will or will not accept from our intuition. But what it doesn't give us is a method for how to reason well. And that is because it doesn't correlate to how we use the word "true" and isn't based on a path of abstraction, and hence we can have no confidence in it, no reason to think that it will lead us to truths rather than falsehoods.

The reasons for our intuitions matter. Why we accept the law of excluded middle, or the rule of existential generalization, or *modus ponens* matters and must be taken into account in deciding whether her theory is compatible with that. It isn't just the linguistic phrase we accept but that phrase as meaningful.

Conclusion

One reason Keefe gives for accepting her theory of vagueness is that it is better than any of the other theories of vagueness she has investigated, at least according to her analysis of those theories. And the reason it is the best is because of its good consequences. In the end, we return to the quotation by Keefe with which we began:

> We do not need a prior justification of the use of the apparatus independent of the account it delivers. p. 192

I hope to have shown that we do indeed need a justification in terms of the assumptions behind the theory, both metaphysical and pragmatic, and in terms of a path of abstraction, in order for us to adopt Keefe's or anyone's model of how to reason well. Keefe's work has given us no good reason to think we need rules for how to reason with vague sentences and much reason to think we are right to cast such sentences out when we reason or else treat them as false.

NOTES

1. (p. 130) Jack Birner in *The Cambridge Controversies in Capital Theory* says:

> It is quite common to use "theory" for a set of abstract propositions and "model" for a set of propositions on a lower level of abstraction. . . . [T]he question of whether or not something is called a theory or a model is mostly a matter of convention. What matters is how theories or models of different degrees of idealization are related, i.e. their relative levels of abstraction. Therefore, I will use "theory" and "model" interchangeably.

2. (p. 130) See "Subjective Claims" in *The Fundamentals of Argument Analysis* for a comparison of the use of judgment, personal standards, and subjective criteria.

3. (p. 133) Some linguists mean to describe as well our abilities to generate new sentences, predicting as well as describing. Such work would be a theory.

4. (p. 134) For a fuller discussion see "Experiments" in *Reasoning in Science and Mathematics* in this series.

5. (p. 135) E. H. Gombrich says in *Art and Illusion*:

> The whole idea of the "imitation of nature," of "idealization," or of "abstraction" rests on the assumption that what comes first are "sense impressions" that are subsequently elaborated, distorted, or generalized. p. 28

Such an idea of abstraction, as he explains, is clearly wrong. When I talk about abstraction, I am assuming that we already have organized our sense impressions according to the usual categories of experience given in our language, or perhaps our biology, or in a particular discipline like physics, or aesthetics. The abstraction is then from that as given. There is no "abstraction" to get those categories. As Gombrich says:

> The schema is not a process of "abstraction," of a tendency to "simplify"; it represents the first approximate, loose category which is gradually tightened to fit the form it is to reproduce. p. 74

6. (p. 136) One colleague suggested that the logic examples all have to do with the structure of sentences, whereas with scientific or ethical theories we are concerned with their content. But the assumption that the world is made up of things is not about the structure of sentences; it is a guide to what structure we will pay attention to.

7. (p. 140) Paraconsistent logics in which contradictions are accepted have been proposed, but they are not given clear enough semantic justification to have been adopted except for some philosophical analyses. In "Paraconsistent

Logics with Simple Semantics" I show how we can reason with contradictory data by isolating the contradictions without supposing that contradictions are acceptable.

Graham Priest in "What Is So Bad about Contradictions?" argues that a claim can be both true and false and that there are true contradictions. But he does so without ever saying what he means by "true." And the three-valued paraconsistent logic he proposes has a true/false division that is a dichotomy in the same way as all other many-valued logics: claims with a designated value versus those with an undesignated value.

8. (p. 142) In "Explanations" in *Cause and Effect, Conditionals, Explanations* in this series, I give a full analysis of why inference to the best explanation is fallacious. One recent example will have to suffice here. In New Mexico, especially along rivers, like where I have a ranch, there are many dense stands of salt cedar (tamarisk). Those trees were introduced from Australia to stop river banks from eroding. Now they need to be eradicated, for nothing else grows or lives where they do and they use an extraordinary amount of water that cannot be spared in the desert. I cleared those trees off a large piece of my land. In the spring a few resprouts must be cut down, which I set out to do this year. Afterwards I told my granddaughter that it was strange that after I cleared an area and went to cut down the trees in another, when I returned to the first part a half-hour later I found three or four more medium-sized trees that I needed to cut. I told her it was because these trees grow very, very fast. She said that was ridiculous. It was because I had missed those the first time around. My explanation is both more general and explains a great deal more than hers. In particular, from it we can see why it is so difficult for ranchers and farmers to eradicate these trees. But everyone (except me) takes hers to be a better explanation because it is more plausible. If we had doubts about which is more plausible, we could amass evidence for one or the other by observing places where the trees grow and by watching me cut down trees.

To judge one explanation as better than another we have to compare the plausibility of their assumptions, which we do independently of the explanation. So reasoning by inference to the best explanation adds nothing; it is reasoning backwards, from conclusion(s) to premise.

9. (p. 142) See Norman Daniels' "Reflective Equilibrium" for a history and survey of the method of reflective equilibrium.

10. (p. 145) Arne Naess in *"Truth" as Conceived by Those Who Are Not Professional Philosophers* debunks all the talk that philosophers make about what the common notion of truth is, about what ordinary folks believe. He does a sociological experiment, questioning people about their views, and shows that there is not only no unanimity but a huge variety of views of truth all held by an equally small percentage of people he surveyed.

11. (p. 153) See my *The Internal Structure of Predicates and Names with an Analysis of Reasoning about Process*.

12. (p. 153) See "Truth in Reasoning" in this volume as well as my *Critical Thinking*.

13. (p. 155) See my *Predicate Logic* for the motive and way in which the assumption that the object language and metalanguage are distinct are used in the foundations of predicate logic. Anil Gupta in "Truth and Paradox" shows that much of the metalanguage can be incorporated within the object language so long as certain kinds of self-reference are avoided, which would certainly be the case for the predicates that Keefe uses as examples. In Chapter XXII of *Classical Mathematical Logic*, building on the work of Buridan, I show how we do not need the distinction between logic and metalogic even to resolve the liar paradox.

14. (p. 157) See Chapter V of my *Predicate Logic*.

Rationality

Except for a clear minimal notion of rationality, the use of that term is too vague to be helpful and can be replaced with other common terms that are clearer. Generally, the ascription of rationality or irrationality is a value judgment and not a tool of analysis.

"He's just irrational to say that." "She's acting irrationally." "That tribe holds irrational beliefs." "Scientists are eminently rational, and the perfect scientist would be the perfectly rational person."

Many discussions of reasoning and descriptions of people or peoples invoke some notion of rationality. It would seem that such a notion is central to those discussions. Yet rarely is "rational" defined or explained.[1]

Beliefs
Rationality is connected with beliefs. Even when behavior is deemed rational or irrational, it is because of some relation the behavior has to beliefs. There are at least three broad notions of belief that lead to different notions of rationality.

Conscious belief: a consciously held attitude to a claim
A conscious belief occurs when someone (or something?) thinks consciously that a particular claim is true. So right now Desidério Murcho believes that Cedar City is in the United States (I just asked him).[2]

Even assuming that a person continues to hold once-conscious beliefs, a person can hold only a small number of them.

Nonlinguistic belief

If we wish to ascribe belief to, say, dogs, then, since we have no evidence that dogs have a language or any notion of claim, we must understand belief in some other sense. It is unclear to me what exactly that other sense is.[3]

Such beliefs are typically inferred from the behavior of animals, but it is not clear whether there must be something more than the behavior to count as a belief. Perhaps a disposition to a behavior of a certain kind is meant. But typically those who discuss such beliefs speak of the thoughts of the animals.[4]

It is not clear that there are nonlinguistic beliefs. Some say there are not.[5] In any case, they would not be connected to reasoning in any straightforward way.

Dispositional beliefs

If someone says that he or she believes a claim, then we have good evidence that they would assent to that claim in the future, barring new circumstances they encounter that might make them change their mind. So we would have good evidence that such a person has a particular dispositional belief, too.

On the other hand, let us call someone's dispositional belief that is not and has never been a conscious belief of that person a *purely dispositional belief*. Are there purely dispositional beliefs?

The only evidence we have for them is behavioral, since we cannot introspect them: once we think of the claim, the belief is conscious. That is, one can ascribe a particular purely dispositional belief only to other people, not to oneself. One might, though, say of oneself, "I have purely dispositional beliefs, I just can't point to any particular one." But we would know that about ourselves only by inferring from our past behavior or from a similarity of ourselves to others to whom we ascribe dispositional beliefs. Indeed, we think that a person can hold an infinity of such beliefs, limited only by their complexity and the fertility of our imagination in ascribing beliefs to someone who has never thought of them.

Let's now examine different notions of rationality corresponding to these distinct kinds of belief.

Conscious rationality for reasoning

I take it that if someone recognizes that an argument is good, then it is irrational for him or her to believe the conclusion is false.[6]

But is it rational to believe an argument is good and suspend judgment on the conclusion? Such skepticism should be applied thoroughly, not just to the conclusion. If one accepts that there is good reason to believe the premises of an argument, and that the argument is valid or strong, and that the premises are more plausible than the conclusion, then there is no room left for skepticism about the conclusion.[7] If one were to say that strong rather than valid arguments leave room for skepticism about the conclusion of an argument whose premises we have good reason to believe, then strong arguments are not good by that standard. So I propose the following.

The Mark of Irrationality for Reasoning If someone recognizes that an argument is good, then it is irrational for him or her not to believe the conclusion is true.

This is a mark we can use, for we can inquire of someone whether he or she thinks an argument is good and whether he or she believes the conclusion.[8]

We have a necessary condition for conscious rationality for reasoning, or simply ***rationality***. I suspect it is also sufficient. Note that if this is all there is to rationality, then we cannot say of someone that he or she is rational but only rational with respect to a particular piece of reasoning. Someone may be said to act rationally or irrationally at this time. For a person to be "perfectly rational," he or she would always accept conclusions of arguments that they recognize as good.[9]

Still, "rational" is often used in other ways.[10]

Irrational ≠ ignorant

If someone doesn't know that some claim is true, and he can't supply it in some reasoning, that does not mean he is irrational. If we wish to tie rationality to what one *should* know, then there would be no clear standard of rationality. "But everyone knows that!" Are you sure? Just how much common knowledge is to be assumed?

Irrational ≠ poor reasoner

Can someone who does not use our logical standards be said to be irrational? As A. J. Ayer says, "A rational man is one who makes a proper use of reason."[11]

But then the intuitionist mathematician can claim that all classical mathematicians are irrational. And vice-versa.[12]

Further, few if any of us reason more than rarely according to a clearly enunciated logic. For one thing, a lot of the reasoning we do every day cannot be formalized in a logic that has clear standards.[13]

If we are to say that anyone who does not reason as we do is irrational, then all pyrrhonian skeptics are irrational. They suspend judgment about the bases of logical systems, the claims that are needed to justify why a particular logical standard is correct/should be adopted. They, it seems to me, are not irrational. Someone who is not willing to take a claim on faith is not irrational.

Irrational ≠ stupid
But can't we say that someone who is stupid, who can't master the fundamentals of reasoning, acts irrationally?

I cannot see how to differentiate a stupid person from one who does not accept our logical standards. To the justification of intuitionistic logic, the child, the stupid person, the classical mathematician, and the pyrrhonian skeptic will all reply, "I just don't get it."

Are dogs irrational?
By the mark of irrationality I propose, we cannot say that dogs are irrational. Dogs do not reason according to arguments, or at least we have no reason to believe that a dog ever accepts an argument as good.

So dogs have no (apparent) logical standards. They are like stupid people or pyrrhonian skeptics. Shouldn't we classify them all as irrational?

Rationality then would be a global attribute of a person or creature: the ability to reason, not just in relation to a particular piece of reasoning.[14] Should we then accept as rational anyone who has a clear standard of reasoning, no matter how bizarre? But why not then accept as rational someone who reasons bizarrely by our standards but who has never reflected on his or her standards of argumentation? Do only good logicians reason rationally? Or are we to say that only people who reason and behave as we do are rational, even though we don't always reason perfectly?

Best, perhaps, is to say that "rational" and "irrational" apply only to creatures who use language.[15] Dogs are not irrational; they are *arational*.[16]

Irrational ≠ crazy
Perhaps we could classify someone as irrational who does not believe his own experiences. He sees the sun rise and asks an authority if it's daytime. He asks his wife if the dog that comes to him at the door is their dog. Such a person isn't irrational; he's just crazy.

Irrational ≠ inconsistent
Can't we say that someone who consciously holds inconsistent beliefs is irrational? Certainly, but what does the word "irrational" add to our analysis of the person's beliefs? Nothing that I can see.[17]

The following principle summarizes how I believe rationality can enter into the analysis of someone's reasoning.

The Principle of Rational Discussion   We assume that the other person with whom we are deliberating or whose argument we are reading:
- Knows about the subject under discussion.
- Is able and willing to reason well.
- Is not lying.

If the person does not satisfy these conditions, he or she is not "playing by the rules," and our analysis of his or her reasoning can only serve to demonstrate that. This is the best definition of **rational discussion** I can formulate, one in which all participants satisfy this principle. We explicitly make clear that reasoning well is by *our* standards. When this principle is violated, it seems clearer to me to say that the conditions for rational discussion are not in place than to say that the other person is irrational.[18]

Conscious rationality for behavior
There is one way in which conscious belief is strongly connected to behavior. A *prescriptive claim* is one that says what someone should or should not do.[19] For example, "Dick should close the window," "You should not torture children," "No one should keep a cat as a pet." But just because you should do something, even if you believe you should do it, does not mean that you actually do it.

The Mark of Irrationality for Prescriptions   A person is irrational to believe a prescription and to act consciously in a way that he or she knows is incompatible with it.

This, too, is a mark we can use, for we can inquire of someone whether he or she believes a particular prescriptive claim and recognizes that he or she is acting inconsistently with it.[20]

Note that since this mark is for conscious rationality, the person has to know that he or she is acting in a way that is incompatible with their consciously held belief. For example, someone might believe "You should not harm dogs" and yet give her puppy a square of chocolate every day. Unless she is aware that chocolate is harmful to the puppy, she is not acting irrationally.[21]   Thus, this notion of rationality depends on the notion of rationality for reasoning since it requires of someone that he or she recognizes an inconsistency.

Dispositional rationality

This is rationality that we ascribe to others based on our observations of them in terms of their dispositional beliefs. Those beliefs must include, if we are to analyze them, a dispositional logic as well as dispositional or conscious goals.[22]

Though our analysis of others' actions must assume they hold an underlying, certainly (in part) unconscious logic in order for us to make some sense of what they do, we need not assume the person is actually reasoning. Indeed, if the person is reasoning, then it is conscious rationality that is at issue.

What many discussions of dispositional rationality seem to focus on is whether the person is consistent in his or her dispositional beliefs (and goals) as inferred from his or her actions and whether the person acts consistently with his or her beliefs. I think that what is meant is that the belief we infer from the person's most recent action is consistent with the other dispositional (and conscious) beliefs we ascribe to him or her. I prefer to say, then, that the person *appears to be acting inconsistently with his or her beliefs* or, for short, the person *is apparently acting inconsistently* since this notion of dispositional rationality is so tenuously linked to reasoning.[23]

But typically authors say that a person acts rationally if his beliefs are "by and large" consistent or are consistent "for the most part."[24] This seems like saying my computer is more or less on or an argument is more or less valid. Consistency is absolute: there is no "more or less" to it. Perhaps what would serve here is that a particular dispositional belief is apparently consistent with the few other dispositional beliefs we are paying attention to and ascribe to the person.[25]

Some say that a person is acting irrationally when he or she does something that seems to be not in his or her best interests. That word "seems" is crucial, for it seems *to us* that he or she is not acting in his or her own best interests. But that does not mean that he or she shares our premises or our standards of reasoning. It is difficult to supply missing premises when we do not have the arguer with us to confirm our choices.[26] It is much more difficult to supply whole arguments for someone who is simply acting.

Often people speak of "apparently irrational beliefs" when they mean the beliefs apparently are not founded on good reasons. That is, *the person could not give a good argument for his or her belief.* But if that is the standard of irrationality, then almost all of us, almost all the time, would be irrational. Alternatively, we might understand it to mean that *we* cannot give a good argument for the person's belief, based on the other beliefs we attribute to him or her, which would have to include their ability to reason well. And that tells us more about our understanding of the other person than about the other person's ability to reason or hold well-founded beliefs.[27]

Conclusion

I, too, would like to label some people I know as irrational based on what they do. After all, I am quite rational, and it always surprises me how irrational others are and how often I have to say to them "Be rational: agree with me." But to differentiate that from simply labeling them "stupid" or "bad reasoner" (or just not liking what they do), I should be able to state: 1. A minimum level of knowledge, 2. The norms of reasoning that I accept, and 3. Rules for how to infer not only beliefs but what forms of reasoning a person is using based on what he or she does. That seems very hard. And in the end, the label "rational" or "irrational" seems to add no more to such an analysis than a value judgment.[28]

This is not to deny the importance of our daily attempts to understand others by ascribing beliefs to them. And often enough we have practical success. But nothing in that success requires or is made clearer by adding the label "rational."

Appendix: Irrational emotions

"Zoe has an irrational fear of spiders."

We hear comments like this all the time. What does it mean?

If "rationality" in this case has something to do with reasoning, then it must mean that Zoe doesn't have a good argument for being afraid of spiders or at least can't recognize that she has no good argument. She just gets afraid of them whenever she sees them, however harmless they are and however easy it would be to swat them with a newspaper.

Or perhaps it means that Dick has told her patiently, time and again, that there's no good reason to be afraid of spiders. He's given good arguments against being afraid of spiders, and Zoe even recognizes that they're good, so she believes that she shouldn't be afraid of spiders. But she's still afraid of them. So, it seems, she has the Mark of Irrationality for Prescriptions.

But this is to suppose that Zoe has the ability not to be afraid of spiders. She *should* be not afraid, and with that "should" comes "is able to." [29] Yet that is exactly what doesn't happen with Zoe: it's not under her control. She just gets afraid, wildly afraid.

Emotions are not under our control, or only loosely so for mild emotions. Perhaps we can train ourselves, with great effort, not to have a certain kind of emotion in a particular situation, like the young man who learns not to feel joy when he sees a girl he loves who rejected him because he's found it leads to unhappiness later. But strong emotions "grip us," we are "in the sway" of them, we are "carried away" with them.[30]

Zoe may have no justification for her fear of spiders. She may have seen good arguments that show spiders are no danger to her, and she even acknowledges that they are good arguments. But for this to justify our calling her "irrational," it must be that she is able not to have the emotion in those circumstances: whether to have the emotion or not has to be under the control of her reasoning abilities. And that is exactly what isn't the case.

Anyway, it's more likely that Zoe looks at Dick's argument and says it's not good. All Dick has shown is "There is very little, almost no chance of being hurt by a spider here." That little chance is enough for her, as she says, "There can never be an excess of caution in avoiding spiders." She is valuing the goal of avoiding getting hurt by spiders much more highly than Dick does. Her aims and the values she places on them have to be factored into her evaluation of "You should not be afraid of spiders."

It doesn't seem that "rational" or "irrational" as epithets concerning reasoning apply to people having emotions. At best we can say that having a strong emotion such as Zoe being afraid of spiders is not a feeling or action that Zoe can control with her reasoning. But that doesn't say much. Any time we have a strong emotion, we can't control that by reasoning. We don't reason to our emotions, we just have them. We can best describe the situation with Zoe as: Zoe is afraid of spiders, and she doesn't have any good reason to believe they are really harmful to her. Adding "irrational" to that description hardly improves it.[31]

NOTES

1. (p. 165) For example, Michael E. Bratman in *Intention, Plans, and Practical Reason* uses rationality as a key concept in his analysis of intentions and planning:

> My intention must *somehow* influence my later action; otherwise why bother today to form an intention about tomorrow? It will be suggested that, once formed, my intention today to take a United flight tomorrow will persist until tomorrow and then guide what will then be present action. But presumably such an intention is not irrevocable between today and tomorrow. Such irrevocability would clearly be irrational; after all, things change and we do not always correctly anticipate the future. But this suggests that tomorrow I should continue to take the United flight only if it would be rational of me then to form such an intention from scratch. But then why should I bother deciding today what to do tomorrow? So it seems that future-directed intentions will be (1) metaphysically objectionable (since they involve action at a distance), or (2) rationally objectionable (since they are irrevocable), or (3) just a waste of time. p. 5

But nothing in this passage or later in his book makes clear what notion of rationality (among the many considered in this paper) he is invoking.

2. (p. 165) See "Truth and Reasoning" in this volume for a definition and discussion of the notion of claim.

Such beliefs are sometimes called "occurrent beliefs," though Ronald de Sousa in "How to Give a Piece of Your Mind: Or, the Logic of Belief and Assent" distinguishes those two notions.

3. (p. 166) Norman Malcolm in "Thoughtless Brutes" says animals have beliefs. Others disagree, and there is little consensus in this area. See Gabriel Segal "Belief (2): Epistemology" for a discussion and survey. Ronald de Sousa in "How to Give a Piece of Your Mind" says:

> In reporting someone's beliefs in indirect discourse our latitude is limited by the canons of acceptable paraphrase; but in the case of animals and infants, it is limited only by explanatory or descriptive purposes for which the ascription is made. And this is not due to the limitations on our access to the beliefs of dumb creatures, but to the fact that they do not have specific beliefs. Only sentences can specify beliefs, and a belief need not be specific at all until it has been formulated. pp. 61–62

4. (p. 166) But see Jonathan Bennett *Rationality*. Another kind of non-linguistic belief is suggested by others who take beliefs to be abstract propositions, thoughts, or sets of possible worlds. Those are then correlated in some

manner to the thoughts of persons or things. See Michael Tye, "Beliefs (1): Metaphysics" for a summary of various views. For the discussion here it will be enough to pay attention to linguistic correlates of those kinds of beliefs.

In "Language, Thought, and Meaning" in *Reasoning and Formal Logic* in this series, I set out a conception of thought that can apply to animals. See also "Subjective Claims" by Fred Kroon, William S. Robinson, and me for a discussion of attributing thought to animals.

5. (p. 166) See Donald Davidson, "Rational Animals."

6. (p. 167) As described in Section A.7 of "Reasoning with Prescriptive Claims" in this volume, an *argument* is a collection of claims, one of which is designated the conclusion and the others the premises, that is intended by the person who sets it out to convince someone (possibly himself or herself) that the conclusion is true.

7. (p. 167) These are the conditions for an argument to be good that are discussed in Section A.7 of "Reasoning with Prescriptive Claims" and developed in *The Fundamentals of Argument Analysis*.

8. (p. 167) Compare the analysis of rationality by Robert Nozick in *The Nature of Rationality*:

> I shall propose two rules to govern rational belief: not believing any statement less credible than some incompatible alternative—the intellectual component—but then believing a statement only if the expected utility (or decision-value) of doing so is greater than that of not believing it—the practical component. p. xiv

Even if credibility is allowed to depend on what can be arrived at through reasoning, this is weaker than my standard because it would allow for one to suspend judgment on the conclusion of an argument that he or she deems good. The second part of his definition is discussed below.

Alternatively, we could take the mark of irrationality to be that someone recognizes an argument is good but believes the conclusion is false. That would implicitly require that it is irrational both to believe a claim and not believe it. Since at least Aristotle, this has typically been subsumed under "It is irrational to believe both A and not-A."

One could also define a person to be *semi-irrational* if he or she recognizes that the only argument(s) he or she has for a claim are weak yet still believes the claim. But the person may have good motives to believe the claim and not be able to verbalize them.

One colleague suggested that what I take to be the mark of irrationality is *meta*-irrationality: first you rationally recognize an argument is good, then you irrationally reject it. "Just plain irrationality is not recognizing that a good argument is good in the first place." I consider that below.

9. (p. 167) Roy A. Sorensen in "Rationality as an Absolute Concept" takes rationality to be defined in negative terms: the absence of certain kinds of irrationalities. This is what I do in defining rationality as the lack of the mark of irrationality, though my Principle of Rational Discussion below sets out positive criteria, too. Sorensen's notion of what vices must be avoided to be rational, however, seems similar to defining "fallacy" in terms of lists of fallacies without an underlying analysis of the concept. For example,

> An irrationality is an inefficiency in this system of rules [of thinking] — a bad belief policy. We achieve the goal of getting true beliefs and avoiding false ones by accumulating and processing information. Although a rational man's hunger for new information is limited by its costs, he does gobble up cheap relevant information. A worried picnicker who refuses to check the weather report is irrational because he is giving up a golden opportunity to get germane news. p. 476

I think that it is better to label such a picnicker "willfully ignorant" rather than "irrational."

10. (p. 167) What follows is not meant to be an exhaustive list of views of rationality. For example, John Kekes, "Rationality and Problem Solving," p. 266, says that theories are rational or irrational:

> A theory is rational if it provides a possible solution to the problem the theory was meant to solve, and it is irrational if it fails to do so.

Kekes is discussing something interesting but not, it seems to me, rationality. For a survey on rationality, especially in relation to relativism and the possibility of translation, see Stanley Jeyaraja Tambiah, *Magic, Science, Religion, and the Scope of Rationality*, especially Chapter 6, and Martin Hollis and Stephen Lukes, *Rationality and Relativism*.

11. (p. 168) *Probability and Evidence.* The quotation continues, "and this implies, among other things, that he correctly estimates the strength of evidence."

12. (p. 168) See Walter Carnielli's and my *Computability* for a comparison of the views of intuitionist and constructivist mathematicians versus classical mathematicians.

13. (p. 168) See my "The World as Process" and the essays in *Cause and Effect, Conditionals, Explanations*.

14. (p. 168) Donald Davidson, "Incoherence and Irrationality," believes that there are some universal standards of reasoning by which anyone could be judged, objectively, to be irrational:

> It does not make sense to ask, concerning a creature with propositional attitudes, whether that creature is *in general* rational, whether

its attitudes and intentional actions are in accord with the basic standards of rationality. Rationality, in this primitive sense, is a condition
of having thoughts at all. The question whether the creature
"subscribes" to the principle of continence, or to the logic of the
sentential calculus, or to the principle of total evidence for inductive
reasoning, is not an empirical question. For it is only by interpreting
a creature as largely in accord with these principles that we can
intelligibly attribute propositional attitudes to it, or that we can raise
the question whether it is in some respect irrational. We see then that
my word "subscribe" is misleading. Agents can't *decide* whether or
not to accept the fundamental attributes of rationality: if they are in a
position to decide anything, they have those attributes. p. 352

Davidson invokes a Kantian precondition for thought. But he invokes no evidence that ordinary people or even logicians actually use these principles in
their daily reasoning, no linguistic or anthropological studies. Indeed, many
have rejected classical logic, which Davidson apparently intends; see "Why Are
There So Many Logics?" in *Reasoning and Formal Logic* in this series,
though I suggest there that there may be some forms of propositional reasoning
that underlie all propositional logics. And the principle of total evidence that
Rudolf Carnap presents in *The Logical Foundations of Probability*, p. 211, is
impossible to apply in reasoning in ordinary life. Davidson's views can better
be defended as declaring a standard of irrationality relative to a particular
community of reasoners, as in my Principle of Rational Discussion below.

Jonathan Bennett in *Rationality* says

I use 'rationality' to mean 'whatever it is that humans possess
which marks them off, in respect of intellectual capacity, sharply
and importantly from all other known species'. p. 5

Bennett then, without argument, restricts his attention to human reasoning
abilities (p. 10) and finally characterizes rationality:

The expression of dated and universal judgments is both necessary
and sufficient for rationality, and thus linguistic capacity is necessary
but not sufficient for rationality. p. 94

However, his examples and comments throughout make it clear that he takes as
the archetype of rationality the empiricist who uses the scientific method.

15. (p. 169) De Sousa in "Rational Animals: What the Bravest Lion Won't
Risk" says:

The crucial threshold [for determining rationality] that animals do not
cross consists in our capacity to be *irrational*. And in turn, the
capacity to be irrational rests on our capacity *to speak*.

See also Jonathan Bennett, *Rationality*.

16. (p. 169) Luciano Floridi in "Scepticism and Animal Rationality" presents a history of views of the rationality of dogs that illuminates much of the discussion here.

The papers in Susan Hurley and Matthew Nudds' *Rational Animals?* discuss animal rationality principally in terms of behavioral rationality discussed below.

17. (p. 169) Frank P. Ramsey in *The Foundation of Mathematics and Other Logical Essays* and others take consistency in a very strong form as the criterion of rationality: the person must be an idealized gambler. But as I point out in "Probabilities" in *The Fundamentals of Argument Analysis*, this seems much too strong a standard, certainly much stronger than the Principle of Rational Discussion below.

Somewhat weaker is the use of probability to legislate rationality proposed by Henry E. Kyburg, Jr. in "The Nature of Epistemological Probability":

> The epistemological import of probability is that it is *legislative* for rational belief: if *K* is the set of statements corresponding to my body of knowledge, my degree of belief in a statement *S should* reflect the probability of *S* relative to *K*.   p. 153

But this makes rationality dependent on a notion that is not essential for reasoning, as I discuss in "Probabilities" in *The Fundamentals of Argument Analysis*.

18. (p. 169) For a fuller discussion of this principle and applications of it in argument analysis see *The Fundamentals of Argument Analysis* in this series.

19. (p. 169) See "Reasoning with Prescriptive Claims" in this volume.

20. (p. 170) This notion of rationality depends on understanding what it means to say that a way of acting is inconsistent with a particular prescriptive claim. Roughly, that can be explained by saying that a claim that describes that way of acting is inconsistent with a claim that describes the world in which the prescription is done. For example, "Dick should take the trash out after dinner" and "Dick went to bed directly after dinner" are incompatible since the latter is inconsistent with "Dick takes the trash out after dinner." This is made more precise in "Reasoning with Prescriptive Claims."

21. (p. 170) Chocolate is toxic to dogs and can lead to death—unfortunately of the dog.

22. (p. 170) See, for example, Chapter 5 of Gilbert Ryle, *The Concept of Mind*. Compare also Davidson, "Rational Animals." See also "Reasoning with Prescriptive Claims" in this volume.

23. (p. 170) Charles Taylor in "Rationality" says:

> What do we mean by rationality? We often tend to reach for a
> characterization in formal terms. Rationality can be seen as logical
> consistency, for instance. We can call someone irrational who affirms
> both *p* and not-*p*. By extension, someone who acts flagrantly in
> violation of his own interests, or of his own avowed objectives, can
> be considered irrational.
>
> This can be seen as a possible extension of the case of logical
> inconsistency, because we are imputing to this agent end *E*, and we
> throw in the principle: who wills the end wills the means. And then
> we see him acting to prevent means *M* from eventuating, acting as it
> were on the maxim: let me prevent *M*. Once you spell it out, this
> makes a formal inconsistency.
>
> Can we then understand the irrationality in terms of the notion
> of inconsistency? It might appear so for the following reason: the
> mere fact of having *E* as an end and acting to prevent *M* isn't suffi-
> cient to convict the agent of irrationality. He might not realize that
> the correct description of his end was '*E*'; he might not know that
> *M* was the indispensable means; he might not know that what he was
> now doing was incompatible with *M*. In short, he has to know, in
> some sense, that he is frustrating his own goals, before we are ready
> to call him irrational. Of course, the knowledge we attribute to him
> may be of a rather special kind. He may be unable or unwilling to
> acknowledge the contradiction; but in this case, our imputation of
> irrationality depends on our attributing unconscious knowledge to
> him.
>
> Thus logical inconsistency may seem the core of our concept of
> irrationality, because we think of the person who acts irrationally as
> having the wherewithal to formulate the maxims of his action and
> objectives which are in contradiction with each other.
>
> Possibly inconsistency is enough to explain the accusations of
> irrationality that we bandy around in our civilization. But our con-
> cept of rationality is richer. And this we can see when we consider
> . . . are there standards of rationality that are valid across cultures? p. 87

Taylor then devotes the rest of his paper to this last topic. What seems interesting in the cases he cites are the reasons we give for calling members of
another culture (Azande or 17th century opponents of Galileo) irrational: they
don't know what we know; they don't understand the world as we do; they
don't reason as we do; they don't want to reason as we do; . . . . Calling them
"irrational" doesn't add anything to that analysis and doesn't seem to sum up
such analyses in any useful way but rather clouds what we have learned about

people of those cultures with what amounts to a value judgment. In the end, Taylor comes close to the notion of (conscious) rationality that I propose:

> But incommensurable ways of life seem to raise the question insistently of who is right. It's hard to avoid this, since anyone seriously practising magic in our society would be considered to have lost his grip on reality, and if he continued impervious to counter-arguments, he would be thought less than fully rational. p. 100

Being impervious to counter-arguments amounts to either an inability or unwillingness to reason well (by our standards) or to possessing the mark of irrationality. Compare S. L. Zabell, "Ramsey, Truth, and Probability":

> It is the credibilist view of probability that if you knew what I knew, and I knew what you knew, then you and I would—or at least should—agree. . . . It is an article of faith of no real practical importance. None of us can grasp the totality of our own past history, experience, and information, let alone anyone else's. The goal is impossible: our information cannot be so encapsulated. But we *would* regard a person as irrational if we could not convert him to our viewpoint, no matter *how much* evidence he was provided with. From this perspective, irrationality is the *persistence* in a viewpoint in the face of mounting and cumulative evidence to the contrary. p. 232

24. (p. 170) Jon Elster in *Sour Grapes: Studies in the Subversion of Rationality*:

> The process of belief imputation must be guided by the assumption that they [beliefs of a person] are by and large consistent. p. 4

25. (p. 171) An alternative might be to base our reasoning on a paraconsistent logic, that is, a logic that tolerates local inconsistencies. But even in paraconsistent logics, as I have shown in a few cases in *Propositional Logics*, consistency can be understood as global and 2-valued as in classical logic.

Dan Sperber in "Apparently Rational Beliefsvice-versa" wants to attribute rationality to beliefs:

> A proposition can be paradoxical, counter-intuitive or self-contradictory, but, in and by itself, it cannot be irrational. What can be rational or irrational is what one does with a proposition, for instance asserting it, denying it, entertaining it, using it as a premise in a logical derivation, etc. Thus to decide whether some belief is rational we need to know not only its content but also in which sense it is 'believed'. p. 164

> How exactly 'belief' should be defined is for psychologists to discover. But even without a full characterization, some of the necessary conditions for a belief to be rational can be specified. A belief is not rational

unless it is self-consistent and consistent with other beliefs held simultaneously. p. 165

But why should we pick out one and not another belief to label as "irrational" from a collection that is not consistent? Donald Davidson in "Incoherence and Irrationality," p. 348, gives a reason that I find too vague:

No factual belief *by itself*, no matter how egregious it seems to others, can be held to be irrational. It is only when beliefs are inconsistent with other beliefs according to principles held by the agent himself—in other words, only when there is an inner inconsistency—that there is a clear case of irrationality. . . .

We often do say of a single belief or action or emotion that it is irrational, but I think on reflection it will be found that this is because we assume in these cases that there must be an inner inconsistency. The item we choose to call irrational is apt then to be the one by rejecting which things are most economically brought back into line.

26. (p. 171) Hundreds of examples in *Critical Thinking* and *The Pocket Guide to Critical Thinking* illustrate this.

Richard Feldman in "Rationality, Reliability, and Natural Selection" shows that the examples given by Stephen Stich of attributing irrationality to animals or people by interpreting their actions are not convincing because there are so many other ways to interpret their actions according to better inferences—if, as he notes, the animals (rats, toads) really have any beliefs.

27. (p. 171) For the relation of rationality as the ability to reason vs. rationality as the ability to make decisions, with many references especially to the literature in psychology, see J. St. B. T. Evans, D. E. Over, and K. I. Manktelow, "Reasoning, Decision Making and Rationality." The problem that pervades the writing of psychologists on rationality is that in claiming someone is reasoning badly they offer no explicit standards or at least no justification of what constitutes good reasoning; as an example, see Thomas Gilovich, *How We Know What Isn't So.* Or worse, the psychologists' standards of reasoning are wrong; for instance, J. St. B. T. Evans and D. E. Over say in *Rationality and Reasoning*:

In syllogist reasoning tasks, subjects are presented with two premises and a conclusion. They are instructed to say whether the conclusion follows logically from the premises. They are told that a valid conclusion is one that must be true if the premises are true and that nothing other than the premises is relevant to this judgement. p. 3

They have misstated the criterion of validity, which is: it must be that if the premises are true, the conclusion is true. A subject might take their criterion at face value and classify an argument as invalid if its conclusion isn't necessary.

Stephen Nathanson in *The Ideal of Rationality* relies completely on external evaluations of actions:

> Deliberation is not a necessary condition of a rational action. For example, it can be rational for me to stop at the curb of a busy street prior to crossing even though I have not evaluated this action with respect to my goals, assessed its efficacy as a means, made unbiased and objective judgments, and so on. While this kind of evaluation would yield the conclusion that my action is rational, I need not consciously carry out the evaluation myself in order for my stopping to be rational. The probable results of my stopping or not stopping are the measure of the rationality of my action, and no reference is required to a method criterion of rationality. p. 39

By this standard my dogs are acting rationally all the time. Or at least it seems so to me as I try to interpret the "probable results" of their actions.

Christopher Cherniak in *Minimal Rationality* also looks to actions as the key to rationality. He wishes to lower the standard of what is rational from an ideal reasoner to one who fulfills what he calls the *minimal general rationality condition*:

> If *A* has a particular belief set, *A* would undertake some, but not necessarily all, of those actions that are apparently appropriate.

This criterion would have the consequence that a lot more people, perhaps everyone, would be classified as rational, if we could decide how to apply it.

See also Carl G. Hempel, "Aspects of Scientific Explanation", section 10, for his account of rationality in these terms and the nature of explanations.

Susan Hurley and Matthew Nudds discuss three different notions of rationality in "The Questions of Animal Rationality: Theory and Evidence," pp. 21–22 (italics in original):

> *PP-rationality* is typically adopted by philosophers and cognitive psychologists. On this conception, rationality is exhibited when beliefs or actions are adopted on the basis of appropriate reasons. PP-rationality focuses on the process by which belief or action is arrived at, rather than the outcome of beliefs or actions.

> There is a conception of rationality prevalent in economics according to which behaviour that maximizes expected utility is rational, no matter how it was produced or selected; Kacelnik calls this *E-rationality*.

> A *B-rational* individual is one whose behaviour maximizes its inclusive fitness across a set of evolutionary relevant circumstances. In its emphasis on outcomes rather than processes and on consistency B-rationality is similar to E-rationality. B-rationality entails

E-rationality in relevant circumstances, but goes beyond it to specify that *what* is maximized must be inclusive fitness.

See "Models and Theories" in *Reasoning in Science and Mathematics* in this series for a critique of the notion of rationality in economics.

28. (p. 171) Compare the view described by John Heil in "Belief":

> A different anti-realist tack is taken by Daniel Dennett, who defends an 'instrumentalist' conception of belief. We have a practical interest in regarding certain 'systems' — people, animals, machines, even committees — as rational, as registering, on the whole, what is true and as reasoning in accord with appropriate norms. In so doing, we take up an 'intentionalist stance'. We are, as a result, in a position to make sense of and, within limits, to predict the behaviour of the systems in question. The practical success of this enterprise, however, does not depend on its yielding true descriptions of states and goings-on inside agents.

Allan Gibbard in *Wise Choices*, *Apt Feelings* says he wants to stay close to the ordinary language use of "rational":

> The rational act is what it makes sense to do, the right choice on the occasion. A rational feeling is an apt feeling, a warranted feeling, a way it makes sense to feel about something. The term 'rational' may carry narrower suggestions, but this broad, endorsing reading is the one I need. . . .
>
> . . . To call something rational is to express one's acceptance of norms that permit it. This formula applies to almost anything that can be appraised as rational or irrational — persons aside. It applies to the rationality of actions, and it applies to the rationality of beliefs and feelings. We assess a wide range of things as rational or irrational, and it is puzzling how this can be. The analysis offers an answer. p. 7

A better answer is that we are implicitly attributing rationality to the actor and not to the belief or feeling. To extend the notion of rationality so far is to end up with a word that isn't going to illuminate our discussions.

29. (p. 172) See "Reasoning with Prescriptive Claims" in this volume for conditions for a should-claim to be true.

30. (p. 172) See "The Directedness of Emotions" in *Cause and Effect, Conditionals, Explanations* for a fuller discussion of this.

31. (p. 173) Amélie O. Rorty in "Explaining Emotions" says:

> A person's emotion is irrational if correcting the belief presupposed by the emotion fails to change it appropriately *or* if the person uncharacteristically resists considerations that would normally lead

him to correct the belief. But an emotion can be irrational even if the presupposed belief is true; for the true belief presupposed by the emotion need not be its cause, even when the person does genuinely hold it. The emotion may be caused by beliefs or attitudes that bear no relation to the belief that would rationalize it, quite independently of whether the person does in fact also have the rationalizing belief. The rationality or irrationality of an emotion is a function of the relation between its causes and the beliefs that are taken to justify it. But irrational emotions can sometimes be perfectly appropriate to the situation in which they occur; and an emotion can be inappropriate when there is no irrationality (if, for instance, it is too strong or too weak, out of balance with other emotions that are appropriate). Both judgments of rationality and of appropriateness involve conceptions of normality that have normative force. Disagreements about the classification of an emotion often disguise disagreements about what is wholesome or right. p. 123

But what is a belief presupposed by an emotion? Presupposed by whom? See "The Directedness of Emotions" in *Cause and Effect, Conditionals, Explanations* in this series where that issue is discussed in the context of trying to clarify the distinction between a cause and an object of an emotion. I think Rorty has it right in her last sentence: it isn't rationality that is at issue with emotions, but whether an emotion is right, or wholesome, or prevents the fulfillment of other aims the person holds as highly.

Bibliography

Page references are to the most recent publication cited unless noted otherwise. *Italics* in quotations are in the original source.

ANDERSON, Alan Ross
　　1958　A Reduction of Deontic Logic to Alethic Modal Logic
　　　　　　Mind, New Series, vol. 67, pp. 100–103.

ÅQVIST, Lennart
　　1984　Deontic Logic
　　　　　　In *Handbook of Philosophical Logic, Vol. II Extensions of Classical Logic*, eds. D. Gabbay and F. Guenther, D. Reidel Publishing Co.

ARISTOTLE
　　1928　*De Interpretatione*
　　　　　　Trans. E.M. Edghill, Oxford Clarendon Press. Also in *The Basic Works of Aristotle*, ed. Richard McKeon, Random House, 1941.

AYER, A. J.
　　1972　*Probability and Evidence: An Analysis of the Foundations and Structure of Knowledge*
　　　　　　Colombia University Press.

BAIER, Kurt
　　1958　*The Moral Point of View: A Rational Basis of Ethics*
　　　　　　Cornell University Press.

BENNETT, Jonathan
　　1964　*Rationality: An Essay towards an Analysis*
　　　　　　Routledge. Reprinted 1989 with a new preface, Hackett.

BERLIN, Isaiah
　　1939　Verification
　　　　　　Proceedings of the Aristotelian Society, Vol. 39, pp. 225–248
　　　　　　Reprinted in *The Theory of Meaning*, ed. G.H.R. Parkinson, Oxford University Press, 1978, pp. 15–34.

BIRNER, Jack
　　2002　*The Cambridge Controversies in Capital Theory*
　　　　　　Routledge.

BLACK, Max
　　1964　The Gap Between 'Is' and 'Should'
　　　　　　The Philosophical Review, vol. 73, pp. 165–181.

BRATMAN, Michael
　　1987　*Intention, Plans, and Practical Reason*
　　　　　　Harvard University Press.

BROADIE, Alexander
   1987   *Introduction to Medieval Logic*
         Oxford University Press.
CARNAP, Rudolf
   1950   *Logical Foundations of Probability*
         University of Chicago Press.
CHERNIAK, Christopher
   1986   *Minimal Rationality*
         MIT Press.
DANCY, Jonathan
   1992   Moral Epistemology
         In *A Companion to Epistemology*, ed. Jonathan Dancy and Ernest
         Sosa, Blackwell, pp. 286–291.
DANIELS, Norman
   2011   Reflective Equilibrium
         Stanford Encyclopedia of Philosophy, revised January 12, 2011, at
         <http://plato.stanford.edu/entries/reflective-equilibrium/>.
DAVIDSON, Donald
   1982   Rational Animals
         Dialectica, vol. 36, pp. 318–327. Reprinted in *Actions and Events,*
         eds. E. Lepore and B. P. McLaughlin, Basil Blackwell, 1985.
   1985   Incoherence and Irrationality
         Dialectica, vol. 39, pp. 345–354.
DE SOUSA, Ronald
   1971   How to Give a Piece of Your Mind: Or, the Logic of Belief and Assent
         Review of Metaphysics, XXV, pp. 52–79.
   2004   Rational Animals: What the Bravest Lion Won't Risk
         Croatian Journal of Philosophy IV-2, pp. 365–386.
DUMMETT, Michael
   1977   *Elements of Intuitionism*
         Oxford University Press.
ELSTER, Jon
   1983   *Sour Grapes: Studies in the Subversion of Rationality*
         Cambridge University Press.
EPSTEIN, Richard L.
   1990   *Propositional Logics*
         Kluwer. 3rd edition, Advanced Reasoning Forum, 2012.
   1992   A Theory of Truth Based on a Medieval Solution to the Liar Paradox
         History and Philosophy of Logic, vol. 13, pp. 149-177.
   1994   *Predicate Logic*
         Oxford University Press. Advanced Reasoning Forum, 2012.

1998   *Critical Thinking*
       4th edition with Michael Rooney, Advanced Reasoning Forum, 2013.
1999   *The Pocket Guide to Critical Thinking*
       Wadsworth, 1999. 4th edition, 2011, Advanced Reasoning Forum.
2001   *Five Ways of Saying "Therefore"*
       Wadsworth.
2005   Paraconsistent Logics with Simple Semantics
       Logique et Analyse, vol. 189–192, pp. 189–207.
2006   *Classical Mathematical Logic*
       Princeton University Press.
2010   *The Internal Structure of Predicates and Names with an Analysis of Reasoning about the World as Process*
       Typescript, available at <www.AdvancedReasoningForum.org>.
2011A *Cause and Effect, Conditionals, Explanations*
       Advanced Reasoning Forum.
2011B *Reasoning in Science and Mathematics*
       Advanced Reasoning Forum.
2013A *The Fundamentals of Argument Analysis*
       Advanced Reasoning Forum.
2013B *Reasoning and Formal Logic*
       Advanced Reasoning Forum.
EPSTEIN, Richard L. and Walter A. CARNIELLI
1989   *Computability: Computable Functions, Logic, and the Foundations of Mathematics*
       Wadsworth & Brooks/Cole. 3rd ed., ARF, 2008.
EPSTEIN, Richard L. , Fred KROON, and William S. ROBINSON
2012   Subjective Claims
       To appear in EPSTEIN, 2013A.
EVANS, J. St. B. T. and D. E. OVER
1996   *Rationality and Reasoning*
       Psychology Press.
EVANS, J.St.B.T. and D.E. OVER and K.I. MANKTELOW
1993   Reasoning, Decision Making and Rationality
       Cognition, vol. 49, pp. 165–187.
FELDMAN, Richard
1988   Rationality, Reliability, and Natural Selection
       Philosophy of Science, vol. 55, pp. 218–277.
FLORIDI, Luciano
1997   Scepticism and Animal Rationality: The Fortune of Chrysippus' Dog in the History of Western Thought
       Archiv für Geschichte der Philosophie 79, 27-57.

FREGE, Gottlob
1918   Der Gedanke: eine logische Untersuchung
       Beträge zur Philosophie des deutschen Idealismus, vol. 1, pp. 58– 77.
       Trans. by A. M. and Marcelle Quinton, as "The Thought: A Logical
       Inquiry," *Mind*, (n.s.) vol. 65, pp. 289–311; reprinted in *Philosophical
       Logic,* ed. P. F. Strawson, Oxford U. Press, 1967, pp. 17–38.
1918   Die Verneinung. Eine logische Untersuchung
       Beiträge zur Philosophie des deutschen Idealismus, vol. 1, pp.
       143–157. Trans. as "Negation" by P.T. Geach in *Translations from
       the Philosophical Writings of Gottlob Frege*, Basil Blackwell, 1970.
GIBBARD, Allan
1990   *Wise Choices, Apt Feelings*
       Harvard University Press.
GIGERENZER, Gerd
2006   Bounded and Rational
       In *Contemporary Debates in Cognitive Science*, ed. R. J. Stainton,
       Blackwell, pp. 115–133.
GILOVICH, Thomas
1993   *How We Know What Isn't So*
       Free Press.
GOMBRICH, E.H.
1961   *Art and Illusion*
       2nd edition, Princeton University Press.
GOULD, James L. and Carol Grant GOULD
1994   *The Animal Mind*
       Scientific American Library.
GUPTA, Anil
1982   Truth and paradox
       Journal of Philosophical Logic, vol. 11, pp. 1–60.
GUTTENPLAN, S. ed.
1994   *A Companion to the Philosophy of Mind,* ed. S. Guttenplan,
       Blackwell.
HEIL, John
1992   Belief
       In *A Companion to Epistemology*, eds. Jonathan Dancy and Ernest
       Sosa, Blackwell, pp. 45–48.
HEMPEL, Carl G.
1965   Aspects of Scientific Explanation
       Chap. 12 of Hempel, *Aspects of Scientific Explanation*, Free Press.
HOLLIS, Martin and Stephen LUKES, eds.
1982   *Rationality and Relativism*
       The MIT Press.

HORTY, John F.
  2001   *Agency and Deontic Logic*
          Oxford University Press.
HUGHES, G.E.
  1982   *John Buridan on Self-Reference*
          Cambridge Univ. Press.
HUME, David
  1739   *A Treatise of Human Nature*
          Edition 1888, ed. L. A. Selby-Bigge, Oxford Univ. Press.
HURLEY, Susan and Matthew NUDDS
  2006   The Questions of Animal Rationality: Theory and Evidence
          In Hurley and Nudds, eds., *Rational Animals?*, Oxford Univ. Press.
KEEFE, Rosanna
  2000   *Theories of Vagueness*
          Cambridge University Press
KEKES, John
  1977   Rationality and Problem Solving
          Philosophy of the Social Sciences, vol. 7, pp. 351–366.
          Reprinted in J. Agassi and I. C. Jarvie, *Rationality: The Critical
          View*, Martinus Nijhoff Publishers, 1987, pp. 265–279.
KYBURG, Henry E. Jr.
  1983   The Nature of Epistemological Probability
          In Kyburg, *Epistemology and Inference*, Univ. of Minnesota Press.
LaFOLLETE, Hugh, ed.
  2000   *The Blackwell Guide to Ethical Theory*
          Blackwell.
LYNCH, Michael P.
  2009   *Truth as One and Many*
          Oxford University Press.
LYONS, John
  1968   *Introduction to Theoretical Linguistics*
          Cambridge University Press.
MALCOLM, Norman
  1972   Thoughtless Brutes
          *Proceedings and Addresses of the American Philosophical
          Association,* vol. 46, pp. 5–19.
MARCUS, Ruth Barcan
  1980   Moral Dilemmas and Consistency
          The Journal of Philosophy, vol. 77, pp. 121–136.
MATES, Benson
  1996   *The Skeptic Way: Sextus Empiricus'* Outlines of Pyrrhonism
          Cambridge University Press.

MCMAHAN, Jeff
  2000 Moral Intuition
      In LaFOLLETE, pp. 92–110.

MCNAMARA, Paul
  2010 Deontic Logic
      Stanford Encyclopedia of Philosophy accessed at
      <http://plato.stanford/entries/logic~deontic./>, revised April 21, 2010.

NAESS, Arne
  1938 *"Truth" as Conceived by Those Who Are Not Professional*
      Philosophers
      Skrifter utgitt av Det Norske Videnskaps-Akademi i Oslo, II.
      Hist.–Filos. Klasse, 4. Reprinted Advanced Reasoning Forum, 2013.

NATHANSON, Stephen
  1985 *The Ideal of Rationality*
      Humanities Press International, Inc.

NOZICK, Robert
  1993 *The Nature of Rationality*
      Princeton University Press.

PARSONS, Terence
  1970 Some problems concerning the logic of grammatical modifiers
      Synthese, vol. 21, pp. 320–334.
  1990 *Events in the Semantics of English*
      The MIT Press.

PRIEST, Graham
  1998 What Is So Bad about Contradictions?
      The Journal of Philosophy, vol. 95, pp. 410–426.

PRIOR, Arthur
  1960 The Autonomy of Ethics
      Australasian J. of Phil., vol. 38, pp. 199–206, and in Prior, *Papers*
      in Logic and Ethics, Univ. of Massachusetts Press, 1976, pp. 88–96.
  1967 Logic, Deontic
      In *The Encyclopedia of Philosophy*, ed. Paul Edwards, Macmillan &
      The Free Press, pp. 509–513.

QUINN, Philip L.
  2000 Divine Command
      In LaFOLLETE, pp. 53–73.

RACHELS, James
  2000 Naturalism
      In LaFOLLETE, pp. 74–91.

RAMSEY, Frank P.
  1931 *The Foundation of Mathematics and Other Logical Essays*
      ed. by R. B. Braithwaite. Routledge and Kegan Paul.

RORTY, Amélie Oksenberg
   1980   Explaining Emotions
          In *Explaining Emotions*, ed. A. O. Rorty, University of California
          Press, pp. 103–126.
RYLE, Gilbert
   1949   *The Concept of Mind*
          Hutchinson.
SCHMIDTZ, David
   1995   *Rational Choice and Moral Agency*
          Princeton University Press.
SEGAL, Gabriel
   1994   Belief (2): Epistemology
          In GUTTENPLAN.
SMILEY, T. J.
   1976   Comment on 'Does Many-Valued Logic Have Any Use?' by D. Scott
          In *Philosophy of Logic*, ed. S. Körner, University of California
          Press, pp. 74–88.
SORENSEN, Roy
   1991   Rationality as an Absolute Concept
          Philosophy, vol. 66, pp. 473–486.
SPERBER, Dan
   1982   Apparently Rational Beliefs
          In HOLLIS and LUKES, pp. 149–180.
SPINOZA, Benedict de
   1949   *Ethics*
          ed. by James Gutmann, Hafner Press (Macmillan).
TAMBIAH, Stanley Jeyaraja
   1990   *Magic, Science, Religion, and the Scope of Rationality*
          Cambridge University Press.
TAYLOR, Charles
   1982   Rationality
          In HOLLIS AND LUKES, pp. 87–105.
TYE, Michael
   1994   Beliefs (1): Metaphysics
          In GUTTENPLAN.
VAN FRAASSEN, Bas C.
   1973   Values and the Heart's Command
          The Journal of Philosophy, vol. 70, pp. 5–19.
VRANAS, Peter B. M.
   2008   New Foundations for Imperative Logic I: Logical Connectives,
          Consistency, and Quantifiers
          Noûs, vol. 42, pp. 529–572.

WAISMANN, Friedrich

   1945   Verifiability

         Proceedings of the Aristotelian Society, Supp. Vol. 19, 1945, pp. 119–150. Reprinted in *The Theory of Meaning* ed. G.H.R. Parkinson, Oxford Univ. Press, 1968, pp. 33–60.

   1968   How I See Philosophy

         In *How I See Philosophy*, Macmillan, pp. 1–38.

WHITE, Alan R.

   1970   *Truth*

         Anchor Books, Doubleday & Company.

WILLIAMSON, Colwyn

   1968   Propositions and Abstract Propositions

         In *Studies in Logical Theory,* ed. N. Rescher, *American Philosophical Quarterly,* Monograph no. 2, Basil Blackwell, Oxford.

WRIGHT, Cory D.

   2005   On the Functionalization of Pluralist Approaches to Truth

         Synthese, vol. 145, pp. 1–28.

YOUNG, James O.

   2008   The Coherence Theory of Truth

         The Stanford Encyclopedia of Philosophy, <http://plato.stanford.edu/entries/truth-coherence/>, accessed on 8/8/12.

ZABELL, S. L.

   1991   Ramsey, Truth, and Probability

         Theoria, vol. LVII, pp. 210–238.

Index

italic page numbers indicate
a definition or a quotation

base prescriptive claim, 27–31, *28*, 31–34
    true — yields a good ultimate aim, *91*
    true ultimate prescriptive claim is
        true —, *90*
Basic Rule of Consequence, 24–27,
    25, 81–83
    for different specified aims, *83*
    for same specified aim, *81*
begging the question, *12*
behavior and rationality, 166,
    169–171, 175, 181–183
behavioral evidence, 166
belief,
    conscious, *165*, 167–169, 170
    dispositional, 166, 170–171
    non-linguistic, 166, 174–175.
        See also animals.
    occurrent, 174
    rational, 180–181
Bennett, Jonathan, 174, *177*
Berlin, Isaiah, *124*
Birner, Jack, *161*
Black, Max, 38–*39*, 96
Bratman, Michael E., *174*
Broadie, Alexander, *117*
Buridan, Jean, 124, 163

Carnap, Rudolf, 177
Carnielli, Walter, 176
categorical imperative, 77–78
cause and effect, 48–49
    hypothetical, *49*
Cherniak, Christopher, *182*
chess, 38–39, 61–62, 65
circular preferences, 57
circumstances, given the, *11*
claim(s), 5, 56–57, 104, *111*, 124
    atomic, *22*
    dichotomy of true/false, 8, 108, 110–
        114, 126, 139, 160, 180.
        See also excluded middle; non-
        contradiction; truth, degree of.

claim(s) (continued)
    dilemmas and, 54
    essentially appearance, *37*–38
    future, 56, 114, 120–122
    judgmental, 130–131, 133, 144
    observational, 134
    plausible, *7*
    scheme vs. —, 123
    types, 106–108, *107*
    when is a — true?, 114–115.
        See also descriptive claim;
        prescriptive claim.
classical propositional logic, 129,
    135–137, 141
coherence as basis of truth, 93,
    118, 150
commands, logic of, 93
common cause, 49
communication, 101–104, 117,
    119, 124.
        See also agreement; formal
        language; meaning.
community of reasoners, 58, 123
    rationality and, 167–168, 169.
        See also agreement;
        communication.
comparing actions for fulfilling
    an aim, *49*
comparing options for achieving
    an aim, *51*
compatibility of an action and an
    action or prescription, *14*
compatibility of an aim and action,
    43
complex prescriptive claims, 22,
    69–71
conclusion, *11*
confirming a theory, 141–142
conscious belief, *165*, 167–169, 170
consequences, judging a theory by
    its, 141–142, 144–146,
    154–155, 158, 160

www.ingramcontent.com/pod-product-compliance
Lightning Source LLC
Chambersburg PA
CBHW072220270326
41930CB00010B/1927